IN THE SHADOW OF
THE LIBERATOR

Hugo Chávez and the
transformation of Venezuela

◆

RICHARD GOTT

VERSO

London · New York

First published by Verso 2000
© Richard Gott 2000
All rights reserved

Verso
UK: 6 Meard Street, London W1V 3HR
US: 180 Varick Street, New York, NY 10014–4606

Verso is the imprint of New Left Books

ISBN 1–85984–775–7

British Library Cataloguing in Publication Data
A catalogue record for this book is available from the British Library

Library of Congress Cataloging-in-Publication Data
A catalog record for this book is available from the Library of Congress

Typeset by The Running Head Limited, www.therunninghead.com
Printed by Biddles Ltd, Guildford and King's Lynn

CONTENTS

ACKNOWLEDGEMENTS

First I must thank Tariq Ali and Robin Blackburn at Verso for suggesting that my work on the guerrilla movements in Latin America in the 1960s should be revisited and brought up to date, now that a handful of the guerrillas from those days are in power in Venezuela with Hugo Chávez. They had little difficulty in persuading me to do so. Thanks, too, to Mary-Kay Wilmers, editor of the *London Review of Books*, who added cogently to their persuasions and subsequently allowed me to publish my preliminary findings, which first appeared in her admirable journal.

President Chávez took considerable interest in this book, and I was privileged to have a long interview with him in Caracas, as well as the opportunity to travel in his company into the Venezuelan countryside.

In 1968, when staying in Caracas with the late José Agustín Silva Michelena, the founder of the Centro de Estudios de Desarrollo (Cendes) in Caracas, I was promised an interview with Douglas Bravo, the already legendary guerrilla leader in Falcón state. As so often happens, the contacts were lost and the meeting never took place. I was therefore particularly pleased to meet and talk to Douglas in Caracas some thirty years later in November 1999, a man still involved in the political organization of peasants, although not himself a fan of the Chávez project.

Many other Venezuelans have been of great assistance, and I should like to single out the Venezuelan ambassador in London, Roy Chaderton-Matos, and his cultural attaché, Gloria Carnevali, who first indicated some enthusiasm for the idea of this book, and helped to break the ice in official quarters in Caracas. Dinorah Carnevali, historian of Copei, made me feel at home in Caracas, and gave me unique insights into aspects of the pre-Chávez era.

Dick Parker, professor at the Universidad Central in Caracas and the editor of the *Revista Venezolana de Economía y Ciencias Sociales*, pressed on me innumerable copies of his excellent magazine, which provided me with much useful material.

Few books have been written in English about contemporary Venezuela, but I would like to make special mention of the brilliant account of the pre-Chávez years by Fernando Coroníl, *The Magical State: nature, money and modernity in Venezuela*, published by the University of Chicago Press in 1997, and still unavailable in Spanish.

The excellent collection of interviews recorded by Agustín Blanco Muñoz with Hugo Chávez, before he became president, was also indispensable: *Habla el Comandante*, Testimonios Violentos, Universidad Central de Venezuela, Caracas, 1998.

This book could not have been written without the help and support in Caracas of my old friend and colleague Phil Gunson, and of Eurídice Ledezma, his *compañera*. They provided me with a bed, food, books and contacts, and they kept up a steady stream of advice, not always taken. I benefited enormously from their knowledge and expertise – and affection, which I warmly reciprocate.

In London, Vivien Ashley, my friend and helpmeet, kept the home fires burning while I was away, and gave me great assistance on my return in the task of finishing the project I had so rashly begun.

R.G., Caracas and London
January 2000

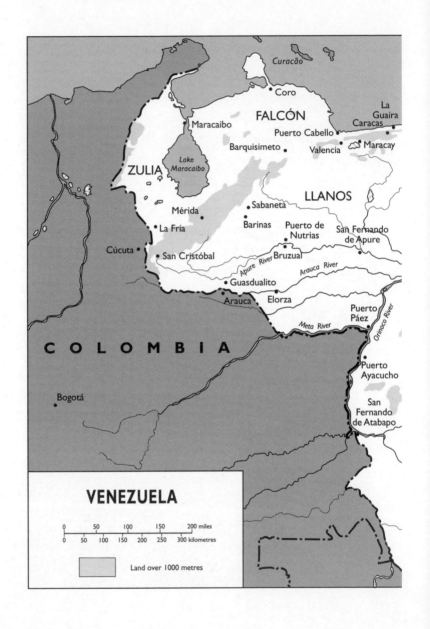

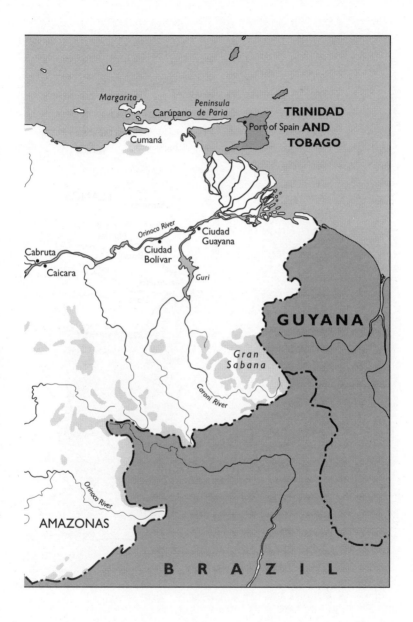

INTRODUCTION: THE RAINS FALL

It would be a harsh God who took out his vengeance on the poorest section of the community.

José Vicente Rangel, December 1999

The mountains of Venezuela rise up almost sheer from the shores of the Caribbean, with gashes of red earth below and vivid green forest above, and the peaks entirely lost in grey cloud. From the aeroplane window I have often liked to imagine this as the land on which the local Indians stood when they first discovered Columbus on their beach in 1498, then, as now, steep and inhospitable, hot and damp – although of course he actually landed some 300 miles to the east, on the Peninsula de Paría, across the water from Trinidad.

The plane often flies along the shoreline before landing, past Naiguata, Macuto and La Guaira, and along to Maiquetía and Catia La Mar, a handful of small and rather grubby resorts with a scattering of high-rise buildings and barely a couple of streets between the mountains and the polluted beaches. The airlines sometimes used to book the hotels there for their overnight passengers, for they lie closer than Caracas, though visitors would occasionally complain of being robbed. I have eaten excellent fish at the road-side open-air restaurants cantilevered over the beach.

When the plane eventually comes roaring in to land, it does so on a tiny ledge scraped out beneath the mountains, parallel to the shore, and you can sometimes catch a glimpse of the shanty towns climbing up the steep ravines. Coming here over the past thirty years or more, I have noticed how a handful of shacks, once crushed in between the hills and the shore, began creeping up the mountainside to form an almost vertical urban panorama.

The rainy season has usually finished by the end of November, so when heavy but intermittent storms struck this coastal area in the middle of December 1999, no one took much notice; they were assumed to be the last fling of a season that was finished. Tropical storms and wayward weather systems are common in the Caribbean and they often cause serious local damage, but it is rare for a provincial disaster to create a national emergency. And on that particular day, Wednesday 15 December 1999, the eyes of the country were fixed on the polling booths, where a referendum was being held to support or reject the new constitution.

Everyone knew there would be a majority for the 'Yes' campaign, backed by the popular and charismatic Hugo Chávez, the former army colonel who had been elected president a year earlier. The only question was the size of the turnout, which might just be affected by the bad weather. People had already been called out to vote five times since November 1998, and even in a country once assumed (perhaps too easily) to be wedded to democratic practices, a referendum whose result was a foregone conclusion must have seemed an unnecessary chore. And it was raining.

Yet President Chávez had called for a respectable vote, and people were happy to satisfy his request. Some 71 per cent voted 'Yes', and 28 per cent voted 'No'. It was a good result for the president, setting the seal on a year of dynamic action and providing his government with the tools to take the country in a new direction.

Then the heavens opened in earnest. Fresh storms brought heavy rain on top of the accumulated waters of previous weeks, causing rivers to rise uncontrollably. In the early morning of Thursday 16 December, the El Avila mountain to the north of Caracas, towering above the coastal resorts by the airport, effectively exploded. Torrents of mud and water on its northern slopes created the land equivalent of a tidal wave. 'Walls of water as high as twenty feet swept down its steep gullies,' reported Phil Gunson for the *Independent*, 'bringing with them whole trees and rocks the size of cars.' All the way along the narrow coastal strip, from Macuto to Catia La Mar, past the airport at Maiquetía, the hills descended into the sea, carrying with them an uncountable cargo of people and houses. In Caracas too the floods brought death and destruction on an unprecedented scale.

Thousands of people were killed and tens of thousands lost their homes. The airport was closed for weeks, and the container port at La Guaira was smashed up completely. 'Dozens of containers were tossed around like cardboard boxes and lie in crumbled heaps,' wrote Gunson. 'Some floated out to sea, and those that did not were looted, along with most of the town's shops.' Despite the predictability of tropical downpours in the area the authorities of the oil-rich nation had permitted a perilous sprawl bereft of adequate water courses, aggravating the natural disaster.

Soon the mudslide was being described as Venezuela's worst natural disaster of the century. An intemperate Catholic bishop implied that it was a judgement of God on the government, but he was reprimanded by the foreign minister, José Vicente Rangel, who said it would be a harsh God who took out his vengeance on the poorest section of the community. Others recalled that the formerly pro-Spanish Church had taken advantage of the famous Caracas earthquake of 1812, in the days of Simón Bolívar, to denounce the actions of the early independence leaders.

The country's National Assembly, elected to draft a new constitution and largely filled with Chávez supporters, was invigorated by the referendum result; it provided the president with emergency powers. Putting on the simple camouflage uniform and red beret that he had worn eight years earlier when leading a military rebellion against the government of the day, he took charge of the rescue operations. To have a former military officer running the country now seemed to be a positive advantage.

Football grounds and stadiums were opened as makeshift accommodation for the homeless, and spare land around army installations were filled with tents. Soldiers manned soup kitchens and started to build houses for refugees on army land. While room might have been found for the homeless on the spacious grounds of the Caracas Country Club, the spiritual retreat of the Venezuelan elite, Chávez was careful not to endanger the national unity created around the tragedy by making political demands on people who might not willingly have accepted them.

Initial reports of the casualty figures were alarmingly high, but a month after the tragedy they had narrowed down to somewhere between 15,000 and 20,000 deaths, with perhaps 100,000 people left homeless. The figures were inevitably vague since, as in most Third World countries, no adequate census has been taken in Venezuela and no proper land registry exists, and no one could count the victims washed out to sea or buried under layers of mud.

We do know that the government acted with considerable competence and speed. When the United States sent out two ships in mid-January, laden with soldiers and earth-moving equipment, the Venezuelans said they wouldn't mind a few bulldozers, but several hundred soldiers might be overdoing it. No one voiced what many people were thinking: how could a self-styled revolutionary government possibly allow imperialist soldiers to make a practice landing on beaches just half an hour from the capital?

For the political earthquake that struck Venezuela just a year earlier is likely to prove of more enduring significance for this part of the world than December's disastrous landslip. When Hugo Chávez came to the presidency in February 1999, an avowedly radical army officer, he was voted in by a handsome majority with the support of a vestigial Communist Party and half a dozen larger leftist groups of varying hues and trajectories. A left-wing revolutionary might seem to be an anachronistic concept at the beginning of the twenty-first century, yet Chávez is just that, a Cromwellian-style soldier who aims to reconstruct his country on entirely new lines.

The electoral victory of Chávez foreshadowed a new era in the history of Latin America. Moving into the Miraflores Palace with a promise to sweep away the ingrained corruption of several decades, he outlined an alternative project for Venezuela – and for Latin America – that would break away from the programme of economic neo-liberalism exported by the United States. He would entrench the power of his new regime by calling for elections to a national constituent assembly that would destroy the ancient congress, and write a new, modernized constitution. He would seek to involve his neighbours in a fresh interpretation of the 'Bolivarian' dream of the nineteenth century, the creation of an independent and 'original' Latin America that would unite its forces against the outside world.

At home, the Chávez government would concentrate on agro-industrial projects and on food production, and on the country's 'endogenous development', the imaginative ambition of Latin America's nationalist left for nearly half a century. Rather than relying on market forces and globalization, the state would actively seek to promote the internal development of the country for the benefit of the great majority of its people, using its own resources and whatever planning mechanisms might be necessary.

In the space of a year, Chávez and his programme have been overwhelmingly endorsed in five elections. In the process he has closed down the Congress and the Supreme Court, abolished the constitution of 1961, and stood back to watch while the country's two principal and long-established political parties committed suicide. At the same time, he has created a Fifth Republic, the first recasting of the mould since 1830; he has caused the constitution to be entirely rewritten; he has given new rights to the country's indigenous population; he has rebuilt the country's judicial system; and he has established a new single chamber National Assembly.

The rewriting of the constitution is less significant than it sounds, though food and drink to constitutional lawyers. Latin American governments regularly give their regimes a new sense of legitimacy by holding a Constituent Assembly that drafts a fresh constitution. Venezuela has not had a new one since 1961, but the subject had been much discussed in political circles for more than ten years. The 1999 version was debated over a period of three months, and will doubtless be found wanting in some respects as a result of this speed. Yet most people were impressed by the serious work that was put into it. Some paragraphs give weight to political decentralization, with more accountability at a local level, but the general drift of the document is towards a more presidentialist system. It also reinforces what is unquestionably a national desire, that the nationalized oil company, Petróleos de Venezuela, should remain in the hands of the state.

For good measure, Chávez persuaded the Constituent Assembly to rename the country 'The Bolivarian Republic of Venezuela', in homage to Venezuela's most distinguished forefather and the Liberator of Latin America, and as an indication of his foreign policy ambition to be a model for the rest of the continent. He has also begun experimenting with ways of integrating the military into civil society.

Reorganizing the country's political superstructure has been seen as a prerequisite to improving the economy, which remains at the lamentable level it was when he took over: unemployment at over 20 per cent; inflation at over 30 per cent; and foreign investment at a standstill. The aim of President Chávez is to dispense with what he always refers to as the policy of 'savage neo-liberalism' imposed by the International Monetary Fund.

Although Chávez has not yet been able to move the country far down this road, one bright light is already shining in the continuing economic darkness. He has successfully secured (with a little help from his partners in Opec) a three-fold increase in the international oil price, from 9 dollars to 27 dollars a barrel. In consequence, and even after the disaster of the December floods, he has a little breathing space.

Chávez has also given a few flamboyant signals to let people know where he stands. In his first year, in October 1999, he travelled to China where, at the grave of Mao Tse-tung, he told the Chinese president that Venezuela was beginning to 'stand up', just as the Chinese people had once 'stood up' fifty years earlier 'under the leadership of the Great Helmsman' himself. In November, during a state visit to Cuba, he played baseball in Havana with a team led by Fidel Castro, and he spoke of how the Venezuelan and the Cuban people now chimed as one, both of them bathing 'in the same sea of happiness'. He has also invited world statesmen of the calibre of Saddam Hussein of Iraq, Muammar Gadafy of Libya, and Mohammed Khatami of Iran to attend a conference of oil-exporting nations in Caracas in the year 2000, to agree a joint strategy for the future.

These flourishes might suggest the hand of a maverick, a Don Quixote tilting at the world's windmills. Yet Chávez is a serious revolutionary trying to carve out a new programme for Latin America. He wants to bring into existence the multi-polar world that the French and the Chinese often talk about, and to show that there is an alternative to the economic consensus that has had such a devastating impact on the poorest populations of the Third World. His message is beginning to be heard in other countries of Latin America, notably in Ecuador, where a radical civilian–military junta took power for five minutes in January 2000 and then rapidly collapsed under intense pressure from the United States.

Chávez is not above harmlessly tweaking the tail of the imperialists. He has refused to allow United States' planes to overfly Venezuelan airspace during their zealous pursuit of Colombian drug traffickers. The American air force has recently been obliged to decamp from its airfields in what was once the Panama Canal Zone, as a result of treaty commitments made more than twenty years ago with General Omar Torríjos, the left-wing commander of the Panamanian National Guard, now dead, who has long been one of Chávez's heroes. The American military have been obliged to make do with staging posts elsewhere in the Caribbean, including Curaçao in the Dutch Antilles, which lies close off the Venezuelan coast.

The Venezuelan refusal to allow American overflying rights is rather more than an irritation. At a time when the United States is about to provide Colombia with US$1.6 billion in military assistance, Venezuela has given clear indications that it disapproves of American policy in the region. In the current peace negotiations being held between the government of Colombia and the guerrilla army of Manuel Marulanda – the veteran leader of the Revolutionary Armed

Forces of Colombia, known as the Farc – the Americans are backing the government; Chávez believes that it is in the interests of Venezuela to lean towards the Marulanda camp, hoping that the end result of the peace talks will be a Farc presence in the Bogotá government.

In recent decades in the late unlamented twentieth century, such 'irresponsible' behaviour by a Latin American government – as in Guatemala, Cuba, the Dominican Republic, Chile and Panama, not to mention Nicaragua – would have merited an American invasion force, an assassination squad, a counter-insurgency team, or at the very least a plot 'to make the economy scream'. Yet nothing untoward has yet happened in Venezuela, although we do not know what plans may yet be under consideration in the deeper recesses of Washington. The end of the Cold War has made it difficult for the Americans to denounce their critics in Latin America as the puppets of Moscow.

President Chávez is a master of the surprise gesture and the rhetorical flourish, and has a considerable sense of theatre. When I was first taken to meet him in January 2000 at La Casona, the presidential residence in Caracas that his rebel troops had once tried to seize, he was standing in the garden with his back to me, gazing out towards the small forest of bamboos and palms fringing the far end of the lawn. Since he is on television most days of the week, making impromptu speeches, greeting protocol visitors at the Miraflores Palace, or glad-handing his way through a flooded shanty town, everyone knows what he looks like. They are familiar with his pugilist's face, his generous lips, his beaming grin, and the almost imperceptible asthmatic tick of his mouth as he takes a breath or is caught searching for a word in mid-rhetorical flow. He always appears decisive and radiates confidence and optimism. Yet alone in the garden he appeared more vulnerable, a monochrome and ambiguous sculpture on a green lawn dressed in a grey suit. He stood absolutely motionless for several minutes, as though gaining strength to face the long day ahead, and seemingly oblivious of the arrival of a stranger. Finally he turned round and walked across the grass to greet me.

I was reminded for a moment of *Yo el Supremo*, 'I the Supreme

One', the magnificent novel by the great Paraguayan writer Augusto Roa Bastos about José Gaspar Rodríguez de Francia, the ascetic Robespierrean president of Paraguay in the early nineteenth century who isolated his country for thirty years from the globalizing currents of his time and laid down the solid foundations of its economic development. Chávez has a similar messianic streak.

The damp heat of the early morning, the lush colours of a tropical garden, and the verandah columns of a building designed as a replica of a colonial hacienda house of the eighteenth century, all conspired to create the illusion of a time warp. Our lengthy conversation – much of it devoted to his plan to reverse the movement of peoples from the countryside into the urban shanty towns – seemed to have a timeless quality to it, as though this was an issue that presidents and colonial viceroys in Latin America had been wrestling with for centuries.

I knew that the December tragedy had demonstrated the urgency of the president's programme, for it was going to enable him to start on his bold plan to move hundreds of thousands of people from the crowded cities of northern Venezuela to new economic centres in the sparsely populated east and south of the country. In these now empty lands he was planning to develop 'integrated' agro-industrial projects that would allow him to cajole people living in the shanty towns to start a new life in the countryside. While early reports indicated that most survivors wanted to cling to their ruined hillside homes, others suggested that some people were thrilled by the prospect of being given new land and new homes – and the possibility of a fresh start. I was anxious to ask him where the truth lay.

Politicians and urban planners have argued for years about what to do with the gigantic urban conglomerations of Latin America, the old capital cities housing millions of people for whom there are few real homes, little food and almost no work. To move urban dwellers back to the country is a tall order, flying in the face of historical experience and of what is now believed to be possible, for few people hanker after the life of the peasant.

In an interview, Chávez becomes a cross between an after-dinner raconteur and a university lecturer giving a tutorial, sometimes telling long stories about distant events, sometimes analysing current problems. I recalled that José Vicente Rangel had told me that Chávez is 'a head-of-state quite unlike any other'. While 'most of them have a laconic style and keep a low profile, Chávez is quite the opposite: he accepts a challenge in any area; he really enjoys permanent confrontation; he is an extrovert and an excellent communicator, and he likes polemic and seeks it out'. Would I be a sufficiently stimulating interviewer, I wondered. Rangel also said that Chávez was much more of an intellectual than people think, with great creativity. 'He is a pragmatic romantic, a mixture of passion with calculation.'

Today we are in tutorial mode, and Chávez delves for my benefit into the history of Venezuela in the twentieth century, explaining how the exploitation of oil in the 1920s had led to the collapse of the rural economy. This had brought an end to Venezuela's old 'balanced and harmonious model', whereby the cultivation of coffee and sugar and cocoa in the country had marched in step with the industrial development of the towns. 'The government simply gave up on the countryside, and what the history books call "the peasant exodus" began.' Chávez emphasizes that 'this was not because the peasants wanted to leave, but because the rural areas were abandoned by the government'.

He uses a personal example close to home. 'This is something that I have felt ever since I was a child; I never wanted to move away from my home village, but I had to go; I was drawn into the city by a centrifugal force.' The aim of his policies now, he says, is 'to make this force go in the opposite direction'.

When he finished sixth grade at his village of Sabaneta, he was obliged to leave. 'If I wanted to continue studying, which I did, and my father was a teacher, then I would have to go to Barinas, which was a larger town, the state capital. But if there had been a secondary school in Sabaneta, I wouldn't have had to go.' When it came to further education, Barinas had no university. 'All my brothers had to travel to the university in Mérida, and I had to come to Caracas, to the military academy. Those who didn't leave, stayed behind and stagnated.'

The same forces that affected education, also influenced the provision of health care. 'People who needed attention had to go to Barquisimeto or Caracas. Even our local sportsmen had to leave. Peasants left when they lost their land to the great haciendas. There was a massive exodus.'

The military were subject to the same centrifugal force. When he was in the army, he says, there was 'always a struggle with the *muchachos* who came from the rural areas to do their obligatory military service. They were brought to the cities, to the barracks in Caracas, and of course when they saw the city – when they set out on a day off – and saw everything that the city has to offer, they didn't want to return to the country. For there they would have no land and no work, nothing, just a shack to go home to. Military service was another factor that helped to force people into the towns.'

Venezuelans have been migrating over many years, Chávez points out, to the narrow centre-north coastal strip of the country. 'Eighty per cent of the population is now concentrated here', he says. All he wants to do, he claims, is to reverse the trend. The principal aim of his revolution 'is to occupy the geographic space of the country in a more harmonious and balanced way'.

There was nothing new about the December tragedy, only its size. 'A hundred people are killed every year when the rains come, and now we've got 15,000. We've been warning people of this for years.' The over-populated northern region, he explains, is not only 'a seismic zone of a quite worrying kind', but it has also seen 'an immense accumulation of people – and children – into *ranchos*', the shanty towns on the hillsides. 'In Caracas there must have been thousands of victims over the last twenty or thirty years, yet no government thought of making an integrated development plan for the country.'

This is Chávez's mastercard, and he has given it much thought.

We already had a project for the country, dealing with its sociopolitical problems and the economy. We had been discussing it in prison, and even before. We had the basic idea of decentralizing the country and dispersing people to embark on a reverse migration – and this is what we are now trying to put into practice. The idea is to strengthen 'lines of reverse migration', in a way that will serve to drive and motivate the decentralizing strategy.

Of course it's not easy. You can't just arrive at a *barrio* and tell the people there that they've got to decamp to the south, and then leave them to get on with it and survive as best they may. No, no, no, it's the task of the state to establish these 'lines of reverse migration', which are really the same as those that brought about the centralizing migration in the first place.

Warming to his theme, he calls for a map to be brought, and stabs vigorously at it with his pencil. 'We will simply put everything into reverse: education will be available, *over there*; health will be available, *over there*; sport will be available, *over there*; land will be made available – so that people can work – *over there.*'

Previous governments, he told me, had made efforts in this direction.

When I was an army captain in the south, in the days of President Jaime Lusinchi, south of the river Arauca on the frontier with Colombia, a settlement was established there that they called 'Pueblo Bolívar'. Along with many others, I always said that this just wasn't going to work. They created a village on the banks of the Arauca, in the middle of summer, and brought people from somewhere quite else. They virtually forced them to come, paying them something to go and live there . . .

Yet it was a wholly artificial place: there was no economic activity of any kind. Look, if this is the town, and all the land around it is *latifundio*, where are these people going to work? In winter, the roads were covered with water; people had neither cattle nor land, and they were given no credit . . . They built a school, but the teacher never turned up. Little by little, people began leaving, to look for a proper life somewhere else.

The solution decided on by the Chávez government, which they hope will be more successful, has been to establish 'integrated centres' of development.

> One of the projects we've been discussing is called Proyecto País, *Poblaciones Agro-Industriales Sustentables* (PAIS) – sustainable agro-industrial settlements – and we are now beginning to put it into operation. We have been working on it since last year, but the catastrophe in December has given us an opportunity to do something more ambitious.
> Last year, to be honest, few people wanted to leave the city, and I told them, 'You are right to have your doubts, because you have been betrayed so often in the past'.

So in its first year, the government began working on a few test cases in various regions of the country, some quite close to Caracas.

> We were looking for lands where we might put up houses and create 'integral farms' – here a farm, here a house, here a warehouse or a micro-enterprise, here a place for people to work, and here a school for the children, with a hospital and doctors and medicine. We wanted somewhere where all these things could be put together, and where people could put down roots . . .

Then came the December catastrophe. 'Now we have at least 100,000 people who have been obliged to move by the forces of nature. This time they know that it's not just words; they realize that they really have been living at great risk; they have experienced death at first hand, and have had to bury members of their families . . .'
The government began to accelerate its existing plans, and Chávez told me of the various projects that were now underway. 'Yesterday we were in Cumaná, handing out houses. All the beaches there are very contaminated, filled with rubbish, and we are making a plan to recuperate them. We've put aside $10 million dollars to clean up the coast. This is a much better zone for a large population

than the coast near Caracas. There's much more room between the mountains and the sea. It's good for fishing, for tourism too, and for agriculture.'

One large site had been identified at the hydro-electric plant at Guri in the east of the country, south of the Orinoco. Houses had been left empty there by the workmen who had built the great dam on the Caroní river. 'I went to talk to the flood victims camped in the Caracas stadium, 10,000 of them, and I told them about Guri. First I had to explain to them where it was. Two of them – and they may have been drunk – immediately said "Yes, we'll go to Guri." Then, after two weeks of a promotional campaign, with photographs and videos, a group went to have a look. I told them to go and have a look and then to come back, and I said that they didn't have to stay if they didn't want to.'

The visit was a great success. 'We have established a community there of perhaps 2,000 people. So many people wanted to go there that we had to apply the brakes. After living through their various personal tragedies, they are now repainting their houses, and remodelling the old apartments that once belonged to the workers that built the dam. They are working there, and even making their own furniture out of local wood, for this is a region of Venezuela with many resources. The children are studying at the secondary school that already existed there. Like almost all the schools in that region, it had many empty lecture halls.'

Workshops have been set up, and the government has been looking around for land. 'Around these houses are 10,000 hectares suitable for agriculture and for fishing, for there's a huge lake created by the dam. Sporting tourism will be possible, indeed tourism of all types, for there are waterfalls nearby and the Gran Sabana, the great savannah. There's a lot of space here, and it's very healthy.'

These are emergency schemes, yet they fit into the wider projects that Chávez has for the country. He knows how important it is to get it right, for Caracas is a powder keg, still ready to explode if things go wrong. Venezuela has been in a state of crisis for as long as anyone can remember. Showplace of a certain kind of democracy in Latin

America for more than three decades and, thanks to its oil wells, notionally one of the continent's wealthiest countries, its unequal income distribution makes it one of the most explosive. The gadarene rush from country to city in the 1970s, followed by the economic stagnation and unemployment of the 1980s, had led by the 1990s to social breakdown.

When I first came to Venezuela years ago, Caracas was a small town circled by relatively friendly '*ranchos*', or makeshift shanties, on the surrounding hills. At night, the lights of the poor twinkled like candles. The wealth and luxury of the city centre, and the poverty and the misery of the *ranchos*, was a dramatic visual reminder of Latin America's most famous characteristic – inequality of income and of opportunity based on deep-seated attitudes of unacknowledged racism.

The middle class is not as large as it once was (a million people pay their electricity bills in Caracas), yet those not squeezed by the economic crisis remain informally convivial, with an international standard of living. Enjoy Saturday lunch in one of the *cervecerías* or beer restaurants of El Rosal or Sabana Grande, and you could easily be in Barcelona, Turin or Frankfurt. Visit the brand-new multi-storey shopping mall at the Centro Sambíl and you could be in any American city of the mid-West. Even at the height of a prolonged economic and political crisis, this is a social group that continues to live extraordinarily well, importing their food and consumer goods from all over the world, though chiefly from the United States, and preferring the cosmopolitan to the national. A country that once exported chocolate now imports Hershey bars.

In more recent years the scale has changed, and the danger inherent in the urban situation has become increasingly obvious. Caracas is now a North American-style metropolis that always looks spectacular. The visitor is greeted by an urban jungle of freeways and concrete intersections, of pedestrianized precincts and shopping malls. A forest of gigantic skyscrapers, in every architectural style, reflects nearly fifty years of unbridled urban development.

Some of the shanty towns have been absorbed and upgraded;

some, from a distance, now have the apparent charm of an Italian hill town. Yet above and beyond, on the sprawling cliffs to the south and east of the city, the shacks of wood and concrete are still growing, stretching over new ground, ring after ring of impoverished suburb and dormitory town. They remain as a permanent and seemingly ineradicable threat to the good life on the valley floor.

There was a time when the hilltop *ranchos* were able to use their height to remind the Venezuelan rich of their existence, but nowadays the construction of skyscrapers has symbolically turned the tables. The great tall blocks in the middle of the city are able to flaunt the wealth of the consumer society over the small hills of misery, while the poor have been driven ever further from the centre.

Like many of the other megacities of Latin America, Caracas is characterized by the virtual absence of law and order. It is a city under siege, with each shopping centre barricaded by fences of steel, each residential street marked off with a guardhouse and a lifting road barrier, and each block of flats protected by armed wardens. The rich live behind high walls with their own private security guards; the youthful poor survive by organizing their own armed gangs. The middle class, sandwiched miserably in between, live in constant fear for their property and their lives.

More than a decade ago, in February 1989, everyone's worst nightmares were realized. The poor from the surrounding hills descended for a week of indiscriminate looting throughout the city. Hundreds of people were killed during the subsequent period of fierce military repression, a reminder to the country of just how thin the veneer of tolerance between the classes had become. The event, soon called the *Caracazo*, had a simple cause: the price of petrol went up; the bus fares went up; and simmering anger turned to active rebellion. The police, on strike at the time for a pay increase, were ill-prepared for an urban riot. When the television began to show people looting in Caracas, and the police standing around and letting it happen, citizens in other cities saw it as an invitation to join in. Even today, more than a decade after those extraordinary and frightening days, Caracas no longer feels really 'safe'.

The country's *ancien régime*, like that of the Soviet Union at the time, had been groping blindly towards new models, and the urban revolt of February 1989 occurred partly because of the movement towards reform. Since the late 1950s, Venezuela had had all the attributes of a one-party state, not unlike those that once existed in Communist Eastern Europe. Its peculiarity, shared with neighbouring Colombia, was that two parties rather than one were given the chance to control the state, turn and turn about. The largest and most significant party, Acción Democrática, had the predominant and hegemonic role, but, to keep up the pretence that Venezuela was 'a democracy', an alternative Christian Democrat party, Copei (Comité de Organización Electoral Independiente), was allowed on occasion to win elections. The two political movements carved out this cynical agreement in the so-called 'Pact of Punto Fijo', signed in 1958, which effectively ensured that other parties, of left or right, would be prevented from ever taking power.

Acción Democrática and Copei both had large memberships. You joined a party to get a job, and to keep it. The party leaders, and the bosses of their tame trade unions, grew accustomed to the perks of power, and particularly to the pickings from the blossoming state industries created from the revenues from oil. Corruption on an almost unimaginable scale became endemic, particularly within the ranks of Acción Democrática but also in the wider banking and commercial community, and it snowballed with the years. The corruption and conspicuous consumption of the Venezuelan political elite became famous throughout the continent. It also created a deep anger within the poorer strata of society, and an unquenchable desire for revenge.

During the boom years of the 1970s, everything had seemingly gone well. President Carlos Andrés Pérez of Acción Democrática, an archetypal Third World leader with a penchant for stealing from the state, ruled from 1974 to 1979, and took the strong statist line that was popular at that time. Shell and Exxon and other foreign oil companies were nationalized, and state money was poured into the development of industry, to the applause of left-wing nationalists everywhere. Such was the flow of oil money in those years that even today there is still much to show for it, mostly in the southern region of Guayana: iron ore extraction, smelting operations, steel and aluminium plants, industrial complexes, and the gigantic hydro-electric dam at Guri on the Caroní river, capable of supplying Venezuela's needs – and those of much of northern Brazil as well.

Yet over the years the state sector began to ossify. It was revealed to be inefficient and uncompetitive, overmanned and corrupt. Short of fresh investment, the great industrial enterprises began to rust away. Projects begun were quickly abandoned. As elsewhere in Latin America, encouraged by greedy international bankers, the country accumulated an immense foreign debt, saddling future generations with the costs of the riotous living of today. In the course of the 1980s, both economically and politically, the country was spiralling towards disaster.

Finally, in 1989, plans were produced to restructure the economy on neo-liberal lines. Returned to power that year with a mandate to revive the atmosphere of the 'good old days' of his earlier presidency, President Pérez unexpectedly changed tack. With no advance warning, his government steered the economy out into the difficult and turbulent waters of the free market, the liberalized economy, and international competition.

The new economic programme soon undermined the established political system, meeting with sustained opposition in the streets and within the ruling parties. The peoples of Latin America, in spite of the surface opulence of the middle-class sectors of the cities, are much closer to the breadline than their counterparts in Eastern Europe. The old party bosses, understandably, were bitterly opposed to this *perestroika*, Venezuelan-style. Quite apart from the inherent difficulty of making the country more competitive, a huge structure of vested interests would have to be dismantled.

In February 1992, three years after the *Caracazo*, Colonel Chávez made his dramatic appearance. A 38-year-old military officer, he promised to overthrow the corrupt politicians, to improve the conditions of the poor, and to move the country onto a fresh course. Then the commanding officer of a parachute regiment in Maracay, an hour's drive from Caracas, he was well positioned to challenge the *ancien régime* by staging a coup.

Although successful in other parts of the country, the attempt to seize the presidential palace in Caracas was a failure. Chávez surrendered and appeared on television to urge his fellow conspirators elsewhere to put down their arms. 'Comrades,' he said, 'unfortunately, for the moment, the objectives that we had set ourselves have not been achieved in the capital', although maybe, he implied, we'll have better luck next time. He called on his comrades to put down their arms.

The phrase 'for the moment', *por ahora*, caught the popular imagination. The aims of the rebellion had not been secured, but most people read his message optimistically, as a sign that Chávez would return to the struggle at a later date. *Por ahora* became his trademark slogan, and the red beret of the parachute regiment became his signature logo. José Vicente Rangel cited this case to me when explaining his conviction that Chávez would always be a strong supporter of press freedom.

> He knows that the word is much more powerful than the gun. He failed when he used the gun, and triumphed when he had access to the media. He spent ten years preparing a coup d'etat that failed militarily; the single minute they allowed him to appear on television was enough to conquer the country.

The effect of his intervention at a time of national disintegration was to turn him into a national hero overnight, celebrated all over the country in poetry and song. In a continent where evangelical sects have been increasing exponentially over the past twenty years, to rival the power and influence of the Catholic Church, the arrival of Colonel Chávez on the scene was greeted as though it were the Second Coming.

Chávez spent two years in prison, but news of the revolutionary project on which he had been working with fellow officers soon leaked out. Resurrecting three South American heroes from the nineteenth century – Bolívar himself, Bolívar's revolutionary teacher, Simón Rodríguez, and Ezequiel Zamora, leader of the peasants against the landed oligarchy in the federal wars of the 1840s and 1850s – Chávez began to sketch the outline of a politics of revolutionary nationalism, destined to have considerable popular appeal. From the country in Latin America that has been most deeply immersed in North American culture and politics, he launched a fierce counter-attack on the programme of globalization imposed on the world by the United States in the aftermath of the Cold War. Soon he was topping the polls of public opinion.

Chávez is a master communicator. He speaks every Sunday morning on his own radio programme, and everyone is familiar with his pedagogic formulations. He talks like a teacher and listens like a teacher, picking up an implicit question and throwing it back at the questioner. On the radio, he is at his didactic best, illustrating, explaining and arguing, with all the sophistry at his command. As the child of two teachers, this is a world with which he has always been familiar, and it is no accident that one of his great nineteenth-century heroes, Simón Rodríguez, organized a radical programme of education for the poor, the Indians and the blacks. It is difficult to overestimate the impact that his broadcasts make on the largest and poorest section of the Venezuelan population.

On television, he will often appear to be speaking to an invited audience immediately in front of him. Then he will suddenly turn, as though to another camera, to address the real audience out there in the rural areas and the shanty towns. It is always an electrifying performance, for he speaks as though he is in instant communion with his own people, the people who understand what he is trying to say and do.

The privileged middle class in Caracas, and a plethora of hostile newspaper columnists, complain about his rough and simple language – he is accused of sounding dull and provincial. They fail to grasp that he is talking to people with whom he has a close rapport, who appreciate what he is doing, and are buoyed up by a feeling of expectancy that something is going to happen, something is going to be done, and that things are going to change. He conveys this sense of excitement in a way that the middle classes are unable to capture, for they are tuned in to a different wave-length. Throughout his first year in office, the old Venezuelan political and cultural elite, grossly overblown by oil rent and petro-dollars, and enmired in corruption, stood back aghast and horrified, hypnotized by the activities of this messianic officer whose interests and preoccupations were not theirs.

Chávez's support comes from the impoverished and politically inarticulate section of society, in the shanty towns of Caracas, and in the great forgotten regions of the interior of the country. He speaks to them every day, in words that they understand, in the vivid, often biblical, language of the evangelical preacher. God and Satan, good and evil, pain and love are the combinations that he often uses. As a result, the mass of the *pueblo* are with Chávez, just as, in other countries of Latin America and at other times, they have been with Perón, with Velasco, with Torríjos, with Allende and with Fidel.

PART ONE

PREPARING FOR POWER

1

NOVEMBER 1999
A GAME OF BASEBALL IN HAVANA

In the name of Cuba and of Venezuela, I appeal for the unity of our two peoples, and of the revolutions that we both lead. Bolívar and Martí, one country united!

Hugo Chávez to Fidel Castro, Havana, November 1999

On a hot evening in November 1999, Comandante Hugo Chávez, aged 43, comes jogging out onto the ground of the Latin American baseball stadium in Havana, followed by his team. Beside him is Comandante Fidel Castro, aged 73, the 'manager' of the Cuban squad. Chávez, the principal 'pitcher' for the Venezuelans, is wearing orange, blue and crimson. Beside him is his wife, Marisabel, a handsome blonde woman with a dazzling smile. Fidel wears a blue jacket and sports a red cap; he is accompanied by his vice-president, Carlos Lage, and his foreign minister, Felipe Pérez Roque, both dressed in Cuban colours.

The event this evening is a friendly match, designed to cement the close links that have developed between the two comandantes of Venezuela and Cuba. It has been agreed beforehand that all the players will be veterans aged over 40, though Fidel has warned of a little 'surprise'. For the thousands of spectators in the Havana stadium – and for the millions watching on television all over Latin America –

this is an historic sporting encounter between two political giants. Fidel Castro is the oldest and most famous revolutionary hero in Latin America in the twentieth century. Hugo Chávez is perceived as 'the new kid on the block' with everything to play for, a radical former army officer whose anti-imperialist rhetoric echoes that of Fidel. His dramatic plans for Venezuela and for Latin America are as wide-ranging as those of the Cuban leader once were.

By an accident of history, the game of baseball, the favourite sport of these two presidents and the national sport of both their countries, is also the preferred game of the United States, the chief imperial power in the region and the champion of the neo-liberal philosophy against which both presidents have directed their rhetoric. The US marines taught the Cubans to play baseball during their long occupa-tion of the island, while the Americans developing the oil industry in and around Lake Maracaibo did the same for the Venezuelans.

Ironically, Che Guevara, an Argentinian, used to argue that the Cuban revolution would never make much headway in Latin America unless the Cubans learnt to play soccer, while Henry Kissinger, of German origin, believed that the future of American hegemony in the continent would depend on the capacity of the United States to adapt to the same game. As it happens, the Cubans and the Venezuelans (and the Nicaraguans) are happy to engage in the demonstrably imperial-ist sport of baseball – and are very good at it.

The baseball-playing Hugo Chávez, elected president of Ven-ezuela in December 1998, soon proved himself to be the most inter-esting and significant figure to have emerged in Latin America since Fidel first marched into history forty years before. Despite their dis-parity in age, the careers of the two men show several similarities. While Fidel led an irregular army of guerrilla soldiers into Havana in January 1959, Colonel Chávez, as he once was, came to power in a comparably unusual way. His unsuccessful coup d'etat in February 1992, against the civilian government of Carlos Andrés Pérez, imme-diately projected him onto the national stage. Just as Fidel Castro became a national hero in Cuba after his failed attempt to seize the Moncada barracks in Santiago de Cuba on 26 July 1953, so too did

Colonel Chávez appear as a national saviour after his failed coup. Moncada, it should be recalled, to illuminate the generational difference between the two men, took place just a year before Chávez was born.

Fidel took power in Cuba in 1958 after a period of prison, exile and a two-year guerrilla war; his defeated predecessor, Fulgencio Batista, fled from the country. Chávez also spent time in prison, two years at San Francisco de Yare, but he took a less spectacular, though no less intriguing, route to the top. Forming his own political movement when released from prison – the Movimiento Quinta Republica, the Fifth Republic Movement – his presidential bid in 1998 was supported by radical nationalist officers and a number of well-known left-wing journalists and intellectuals, many of whom had been supporters of Venezuela's Fidelista guerrilla movement in the 1960s. So corrupt and detested had the existing 'democratic' regime become in Venezuela that Chávez stormed his way through to electoral victory in December 1998 over the ashes of a dismayed and dispirited *ancien régime*. His principal civilian opponent in the 1990s, former President Pérez, while not in exile, was forced to spend time under house arrest facing charges of corruption.

The close friendship of Chávez with Fidel, forged over the years, and celebrated with an official state visit to Havana and a game of baseball, has provided Chávez with incomparable revolutionary credentials – the kind that are recognized in the shanty towns of Venezuela, where the majority of the population lives. But such credentials are not so warmly approved by Venezuela's rich and tiny elite, whose Cuban friends live in Miami not Havana, and whose lives are spent in a permanent state of alarm about their property and their bank accounts.

For the best part of a decade Chávez has sought to stir up the nationalist passions of his country's population with a dose of revolutionary rhetoric long out of fashion both in Latin America and in the rest of the world. He has tried to combat the unquestioning acceptance of neo-liberalism and globalization with the revival of radical nationalism, drawing on the words and actions of Venezuela's pantheon of nineteenth-century heroes. He has exalted the figure of Simón Bolívar in much the same way as Fidel has used the example of the nineteenth-century Cuban patriot José Martí. Bolívar and Martí both fought against the Spanish empire in the nineteenth century, and Fidel and Chávez have revived the memory of those struggles in the twentieth-century campaign against the attempt by the American empire to rule the world.

Chávez took up this theme during his visit to Havana at the time of the baseball game. 'Venezuela is travelling towards the same sea as the Cuban people,' he told an astonished audience at the University of Havana, 'a sea of happiness and of real social justice and peace.' Then turning to Fidel, and calling him 'brother', he enlarged on one of his central themes: the indivisibility of the Latin American revolution:

> Here we are, as alert as ever, Fidel and Hugo, fighting with dignity and courage to defend the interests of our people, and to bring alive the ideas of Bolívar and Martí. In the name of Cuba and of Venezuela, I appeal for the unity of our two peoples, and of the revolutions that we both lead. Bolívar and Martí, one country united!

Castro, who has spent forty years searching for allies on the Latin American mainland, was more than satisfied with the rhetoric. But he had no intention of this newfound friendship standing in the way of winning the baseball game. In the baseball stadium, at the beginning of the sixth game, his promised 'surprise' materialized. Two members of the Cuban reserve were brought on, who turned out to be two of Cuba's most famous young professionals, Oresty Kinderlan and Luís Ulasia. They were disguised with wigs and beards to make them look like veterans, but no one was fooled – although Chávez claimed to have been. With such guerrilla tactics, Cuba won the game without much difficulty, 5–4.

Chávez's visit to Cuba was not just about baseball. Other more serious matters were under consideration. Cuba's long-established sugar-for-oil swap with Russia was scheduled to end in 1999, and the Cubans were hoping that they might now be able to secure Venezuelan oil at preferential rates. There was a precedent for this – under terms of an agreement signed in San José, Costa Rica, some years before, Venezuela and Mexico had agree to provide oil at such rates to 11 countries of the Caribbean and Central America. Cuba was hoping to join this select group.

Meanwhile, in another part of the country, Héctor Ciávaldini, the head of Petróleos de Venezuela, the Venezuelan state oil company, was examining what could be done with Cuba's Cienfuegos oil refinery, built by the Russians in the 1960s and now in a dilapidated condition. The Cubans had expressed hopes that Venezuela might invest US$200 million in the refinery, but the eventual agreement was more modest. Petróleos de Venezuela and Cupet, the Cuban state oil company, would set up a joint company to run the Cienfuegos operation, and Venezuela would supply it with 70,000 barrels a day.

Ciávaldini was asked by journalists what effect this agreement would have on the United States. 'We don't ask questions when the US buys things from China. Thirty per cent of the mass consumption articles that the US imports come from China. If they have these kinds of relationship, I don't think we should feel inhibited from having relations with whoever we want – with China, with Malaysia, or with Cuba.' A week later, Ali Rodríguez Araque, Venezuela's minister of energy and mines, was visiting Saddam Hussein in Baghdad.

Venezuela and Cuba have had a long and troubled interaction over the past half century, and it is appropriate to begin a book about Hugo Chávez with this account of the reconciliation of two countries and two governments. For the radical programme that Chávez embraces today has deep roots in the conflictive events in Latin America of the past 50 years. During that time, revolutionary movements in Venezuela, inspired and directly assisted by Fidel and Che Guevara, sought to spread the revolutionary message of the Cuban revolution from the island to the continent. In 1959, just after his victory over Batista, Fidel visited Caracas to thank the Venezuelans for their moral support. At that moment, he was the most popular man in the country, spontaneously welcomed by thousands of people demonstrating in the great space of El Silencio in the city centre.

Just a year before Fidel's guerrilla victory, there had been a popular uprising in Caracas, in January 1958. A revolt at a military base at Maracay (later to be the base from which Chávez launched his coup in 1992) had been followed by rioting in the capital and the formation of a left-wing 'Patriotic Junta' that called successfully for a general strike. The Venezuelan dictator, Marcos Pérez Jiménez, was forced to resign. Venezuela and Cuba appeared to be moving forward together on parallel tracks.

The eventual beneficiary of the uprising was Rómulo Betancourt, founder of Acción Democrática. He was a reformist politician of great skill and ruthlessness who enjoyed the support of the United States. The Americans viewed Betancourt's Venezuela as a model for Latin America, and set it up as such in opposition to Castro's Cuba. When Fidel came to Caracas to thank the Venezuelan people for the support they had given to his cause, he was cheered to the echo, but for Betancourt, standing at his side, there was only 'a storm of booing'. Betancourt's Venezuela soon became a bastion of the anti-Cuban cause in the Americas; the secret service was handed over to anti-Castro exiles from Miami.

Many left-wing Venezuelans opposed to Betancourt were unhappy about these developments. Following the example of the Cuban revolution, they took to the hills in the early 1960s and organized a guerrilla insurrection that lasted until the end of the decade. Some of the guerrillas came originally from splinter groups from Betancourt's Acción Democrática, others came from the Communist Party. Still others worked hand in glove with radical groups within the armed forces – a significant aspect of these rebellions in the light of subsequent history. Civilian activists from the Communist and other parties took part in two major military revolts against the Acción Democrática government in 1962, at Carúpano and Puerto Cabello. The revolts were unsuccessful but left an indelible memory. In a statement after Carúpano, one of the Communist leaders, Guillermo García Ponce, described the political programme of the rebellious officers as 'far-reaching, nationalistic, and patriotic', and praised it for calling on 'all Venezuelans to work for democratic reconstruction'. The Communist Party, said García Ponce, believed that the rebellious officers had 'done Venezuela a great service'. Nearly four decades later, in 1999, he was a member of the Constituent Assembly supporting Chávez.

Hugo Chávez did not emerge from a vacuum. He is the heir to the revolutionary traditions of the Venezuelan left. Many survivors of the guerrilla insurrection, now in their late sixties, are still participating in politics today, some on the side of Chávez, others in the opposition. Chávez had spent time cultivating the civilian left when planning his coup d'etat, and in government he has drawn on the talents of several people who come from the radical political traditions of the 1960s – and even earlier.

Ali Rodríguez Araque, his minister of energy and mines, who has spearheaded the revival of Opec, was a guerrilla fighter in Falcón state in the 1960s, and later was active in an important left-wing party, La Causa Radical. Lino Martínez, the minister of labour, was also once a guerrilla. Half a dozen former guerrillas can be found among the Chávez supporters in the National Assembly.

Chávez relies particularly on two civilians: Luís Miquilena and José Vicente Rangel. They are close friends and his most intimate political advisers. Both are historic stars in the firmament of the Venezuelan left, and have been around for close on half a century, some of which they have spent in prison or in exile. Rangel, the foreign minister, now aged 70, was the presidential candidate of the left on three occasions. One of the great charmers of Latin American politics, he is an active and vocal defender of the government. Miquilena, the president of the National Assembly, was a leader of the bus drivers' union in Caracas in the 1940s, and the co-founder of an anti-Stalinist Communist Party in 1946. Now a sprightly 83-year-old, he was Chávez's first minister of the interior. He still retains a tough

Leninist streak, which proved useful when he helped construct the political movement of soldiers and civilians – the Fifth Republic Movement – that supported Chávez's election campaign.

Ignácio Arcaya, the minister of the interior, is Miquilena's godson and the son of a former foreign minister who was sacked in 1960 for failing to sign an American-inspired anti-Cuban motion at a meeting of the Organization of American States. Jorge Giordani, the planning minister, was formerly the economic adviser to another left-wing party, the Movement for Socialism, which emerged after the end of the guerrilla rebellion.

Not all the surviving revolutionaries of the 1960s are supporting Chávez. Opposing him from the right is a group of former guerrillas, led by Teodoro Petkoff, once a prominent Communist leader and a prominent minister in the previous government. Petkoff has also on occasion been the presidential candidate of the left, and throughout 1999, he was the influential editor of an evening paper, *El Mundo*, opposed to Chávez. (He was sacked by the paper's proprietor in December.) Among his columnists were a number of guerrilla fighters who had made the journey from Cuban-style socialism to social democracy.

Opposing Chávez from the left is Douglas Bravo, the guerrilla leader in Falcón in the 1960s and perhaps the most well known of the uncompromising leftists of the past. Bravo had collaborated with Chávez on his revolutionary project in the 1980s, on the assumption that it was going to be a genuinely civilian–military operation. He withdrew after 1992 when he felt that civilians were being by-passed, and that Chávez's programme was insufficiently radical.

Years ago, in 1968, I spent a couple of weeks in Caracas awaiting a call to interview Bravo in the hills. As so often used to happen, the summons never came, but some three decades later, in November 1999, I finally caught up with him, and he came to see me in the apartment of a friend. Now in his late sixties, Bravo remains a cheerful and resilient revolutionary, though not in Chávez's camp. He tells me that he used to know Chávez quite well, at a time when the future president was a junior officer conspiring against the government. 'Chávez is an intelligent man,' says Bravo, 'he is bold, charismatic, and an excellent speaker; he has a natural ability to command.'

The old guerrilla also has a few criticisms. Chávez, he says sharply, 'is quite capable of making sudden changes in direction. These can be positive or negative. He can easily make agreements with one group, and then abandon them when he makes a deal with another. This was a very serious characteristic when Chávez was a conspirator, and it is quite dangerous now that he is the President of Venezuela.'

Rangel, the foreign minister, is of the same generation as Bravo but takes a less critical view: 'It's a mistake to demonize Chávez, just as it is an error to sanctify him. If if he had not emerged, there would certainly have been somebody else. Fortunately, this has proved the best way to secure change, peacefully and with civilians. After all, we might easily have had a Pinochet.'

The debate within the Venezuelan left about revolutionary tactics, and about the alliance between soldiers and civilians, has continued into the Chávez era, unremitting and unresolved.

2

THE MILITARY PROMOTIONS OF HUGO CHÁVEZ

What has been called the democratic system in Venezuela has not differed much in recent years from what came before . . . Everything has basically remained the same; it's been the same system of domination with a different face, whether it's that of General Gómez or of Doctor Rafael Caldera . . .

Hugo Chávez interviewed in June 1995

The small, hot town of Barinas stands beneath the last hills of the Andes, the gateway to the great plains of the Orinoco basin. I came here on the bus from Caracas, an eight-hour journey on a good road along the foot of the hills, through Maracay and Carabobo and Acarígua. Here begins the vast expanse of the *llanos*, the low-lying and marshy cattle lands of the centre-south of the country where innumerable rivers make their way down from the Andes to the Orinoco. The *llanos* stretch down to the Colombian frontier and beyond, and eventually reach the tributaries of the Amazon in Brazil.

Barinas spreads out in extensive fashion from its crowded bus station, mostly with single-storey buildings, and I put up at a small hotel in the Plaza Zamora, beside the San Domingo river. The name of the square recalls Ezequiel Zamora, the revolutionary leader of the federal forces in the 1850s, who won a great victory in 1859 not far from here, at the battle of Santa Inés. Zamora has long been one of the heroes from whom President Chávez draws his inspiration. The *llanos* were the scene of many of the other fratricidal battles of the nineteenth century, and in these latitudes Simón Bolívar, another Chávez hero, gathered the plainsmen together for his spirited and successful attack on the Spanish forces in Colombia in 1819.

This is the provincial Latin America that I like the most, only eight hours by bus from the capital city, but light years away by most other measurements. 'There's little to do or see here', says the guidebook, and that's how it should be. I find an open-air restaurant serving barbecued chicken and yucca, and the regional beer from Maracaibo. The walls are covered with utopian murals in lurid colours, with exotic birds flying out of the forest and over a great expanse of water, and the evocative songs of the *llaneros* pour out from an ancient juke-box.

Yet modernity is not altogether absent. Behind the immense statue of Bolívar in the central square stands a gigantic communications mast, tucked in behind the state governor's relatively humble palace. Designed to command all it surveys from a great height, the statue is wholly dwarfed by this essential element of the contemporary world. Even my hotel, appropriately called the 'Hotel Internacional', receives several dozen television programmes plucked from the air, only four of them being generated in Venezuela. The disparity between the respect accorded to the historical figure of Bolívar, and the reality of a twenty-first-century world with technological trappings that were unimaginable two centuries ago, is one of the reasons why some educated Venezuelans still have doubts about the course on which President Chávez has embarked. Invoking the thoughts and ambitions of Bolívar today can seem rather, well, quaint.

I have come to Barinas because this is the home state of the president. His father, Hugo de los Reyes Chávez, has been the governor here since November 1998, and a supporter of his son's political movement. The president was actually born a few miles away, in the large village of Sabaneta, but he came to school in Barinas and was stationed here for some years in the army. It seems an appropriate place to start.

Chávez was born on 28 July 1954. His parents, Hugo de los Reyes Chávez and Elena Frias, were both school-teachers, but they took an active part in political life. His father had long been involved in the educational politics of the state, being enrolled at one stage in the Christian Democrat party, Copei. Politics seems to run in the blood, for as well as Chávez senior being the state governor, his elder brother, Adán Chávez, a professor at the university in Mérida, was a member of the Constituent Assembly in 1999, and also a supporter of his brother's political movement. Such close family links (almost tribal perhaps) are characteristic of life at the top in politics throughout Latin America.

Recent history still lies close to the surface in this region, and the Chávez family is itself the heir to some of the rebellious traditions of the nineteenth century. The great-grandfather of Chávez's father was Colonel Pedro Pérez Pérez, a guerrilla chief from the 1840s. Ezequiel Zamora summoned this Colonel Pérez to join his 'Sovereign Army of the People' and to fight with them against the landed oligarchy. The son of Colonel Pérez, in turn, was another legendary figure, General Pedro Pérez Delgado, known as Maisanta, who rebelled in 1914 against the dictatorship of General Juan Vicente Gómez. Maisanta had originally hitched his star to the fortunes of General Cipriano Castro at the turn of the twentieth century, and had been settled in the *llanos* as Castro's man in Sabaneta. He married a local woman, Claudina Infante, and together they had two daughters, one of whom, Rosa, was the grandmother of Hugo Chávez.

Maisanta subsequently organized a guerrilla movement against Gómez in the *llanos*, but he was captured and his lands were confiscated. He died in prison, but his son continued the struggle. Chávez was told stories by his grandmother of how soldiers had arrived at their farm with machetes to slaughter the peasants and to burn down all the barns and buildings. He was also told, such were the enduring political hatreds of the region, that Maisanta was an assassin, best forgotten. Only when an adult did Chávez understand that his great-grandfather had been a freedom fighter.

This local and personal history had a considerable impact on the youthful Hugo, and he was to return to it in later years when stationed as a young officer in Barinas and at other points in the *llanos*. Maisanta and Ezequiel Zamora, as archetypal soldier-revolutionaries, have remained, alongside Bolívar, as his principal heroes to this day.

Chávez first enrolled as a soldier at the age of 17, in 1971, and he often claims that it was his enthusiasm for baseball that persuaded him to join the army. He was to become one of the army's champion players, though eventually he was to show a greater propensity for politics than for sport. He entered the military academy in Caracas during the first presidency of Rafael Caldera, the founder of Copei, at a time when some of the future supporters of his government were abandoning the guerrilla struggle in the hills. Caldera was to pioneer the pacification of the country after the revolutionary insurrection of the 1960s.

The political thinking of the young Chávez was influenced by his early love of history, sparked off by his family's particular experience, but soon he was to acquire fresh insights into contemporary affairs. In 1974, while still a cadet, he travelled to Peru with a dozen other young soldiers. They had gone to participate in the international celebration of the 150th anniversary of the battle of Ayacucho, held on the Andean battleground outside the old colonial town. The battle, in 1824, had marked the liberation of Peru from Spanish rule by the forces of Bolívar and Sucre. In more recent years, since 1968, Peru had been the scene of a radical experiment in government, conducted by the armed forces. General Juan Velasco Alvarado, a progressive officer, had seized power in Lima in 1968 and embarked on a far-reaching programme of reform, supported by revolutionaries within the armed forces and by Peru's left-wing parties. This was Chávez's first acquaintance with a progressive military regime, and Peru, evocatively for him, was a country where Bolívar still had an honoured name.

Chávez and the other Venezuelan cadets were each given a small memento by President Velasco, a booklet of speeches called 'La Revolución Nacional Peruana'. He still remembers the visit, the booklet and the enthusiastic support that the Peruvian cadets gave their president, and the Peruvian experiment itself made a lasting impression on his own political thinking.

In 1975, a year after his trip to Lima and Ayacucho, Chávez graduated from the military academy as a sub-lieutenant, receiving his sword of command from the hands of President Carlos Andrés Pérez at the annual passing-out parade on 5 July, the anniversary of Venezuelan independence in 1811. President Pérez was the man he was to try to overthrow 16 years later, in February 1992.

Chávez spent the next two years based in Barinas, joining a counter-insurgency battalion that had been stationed there since the guerrilla war of the 1960s. In 1976, the battalion was sent to Cumaná to help crush a fresh guerrilla outbreak organized by a group within Bandera Roja, or Red Flag, one of the ultra-leftist groups that had remained faithful to the old guerrilla strategy of the 1960s. It was at this stage, according to his own account, that Chávez began to feel some sympathy for the guerrillas he was supposed to be fighting. He also became aware for the first time, he says, of how the generalized corruption in the political world was percolating through into the armed forces. Officers would fiddle their budgets and pilfer equipment for their own personal use.

In 1977, at the age of 23 and with only two years' experience as a lieutenant, Chávez decided to form his own armed group, the Ejército de Liberación del Pueblo de Venezuela (ELPV), the Liberation Army of the Venezuelan People. He gathered together a few friends and they dreamed of revolution.

'What was the purpose?' he was asked years later by Gabriel García Márquez. 'It was very simple,' Chávez told him. 'We did it to prepare ourselves in case something should happen.' This was doubtless but the youthful enthusiasm of a 23-year-old, and, as he recalls, 'we hadn't the least idea at that time what we were going to do'. But it was an important pointer to the future.

Not long afterwards, he met another young officer with similarly radical attitudes, Jesús Urdaneta Hernández, who soon became a friend. Chávez told him about the formation of his revolutionary group, and said that he had been disappointed by his experience in the army, for he had not found it to be as he had expected. 'I'm not going to go on like this in the army all my life,' he declared.

Chávez then suggested to Urdaneta that perhaps they should try something different. 'Why don't we create a movement within the army,' he said. 'We're not going to join the guerrillas, that's all over and done with, and anyway our outlook and our education doesn't fit with them.'

What he had in mind, he revealed to Urdaneta, was something entirely different, 'a movement within the armed forces'. Colonel Urdaneta was for many years a faithful ally of Chávez and played a central role in the state as the head of the secret police, the Dirección de Servicios de Inteligencia y Prevención (the Disip). He resigned in January 2000 after revelations about Disip involvement in the shooting of looters after the mudslide disaster of December 1999.

Chávez was transferred in 1978 to a tank battalion in Maracay, and two years after that, pursuing his interests in baseball, he was moved back to the military academy in Caracas as the chief sports instructor. He remained there for five influential years, from 1980 to 1985, eventually graduating from sports to culture and becoming a tutor in history and politics. It is difficult to underestimate the impact that this intelligent and charismatic tutor had on his students in the academy.

During this period the political ambitions of Chávez hardened into a firm belief that his generation of military officers would at some future date be called upon to run the country. By the early 1980s, the glory years of 'Venezuela Saudíta' were over. Those years in the 1970s, when Venezuelans were led to believe that they might soon inhabit a rich and developed Western country, were finally replaced with the harsh reality of devaluation and indebtedness, leading to a worsening spiral of poverty. The civilian leaders began to look increasingly incompetent and vulnerable. The government of Carlos Andrés Pérez in the 1970s had lived off the immensely increased revenues of the post-1973 oil boom and the petro-dollar loans it brought in its train; his successors in the 1980s had nothing so substantial at their command.

Finally, in 1982, Chávez began to organize a serious political conspiracy. Assembling two other military officers, both lecturers at the military academy, he created a political cell within the army, and called it the Movimiento Bolivariano Revolucionario-200 (MBR-200), the Bolivarian Revolutionary Movement. The '200' was added to mark the year-long celebrations that were taking place at that time to record the 200th anniversary of the birth of Bolívar in July 1783. The two other officers were Felipe Acosta Carles and Chávez's old friend Jesús Urdaneta Hernández. While Urdaneta Hernández survived to play an important role in the Chávez government in 1999, Acosta was killed during the *Caracazo* rebellion in 1989.

On 17 December 1982, the revolutionary officers swore an oath underneath the great tree at Samán de Güere, near Maracay, repeating the words of the pledge that Simón Bolívar had made in Rome in 1805, when he swore to devote his life to the liberation of Venezuela from the Spanish yoke: 'I swear before you, and I swear before the God of my fathers, that I will not allow my arm to relax, nor my soul to rest, until I have broken the chains that oppress us . . . '

The Bolivarian Revolutionary Movement started more as a political study circle than as a subversive conspiracy, but as the young officers examined the history and the contemporary problems of their country, they began thinking in terms of some kind of coup d'etat. They knew that they would have to overthrow the existing political system, for they believed that Venezuela's version of 'democracy' was a sham. Interviewed by Agustín Blanco Muñoz in June 1999, Chávez explained his reservations:

What has been called the democratic system in Venezuela has not differed much in recent years from what came before: the dictatorship of Marcos Pérez Jiménez; the three years government [of Acción Democrática] between 1945 and 1948; the governments of Isaías Medina and López Contreras; and even the government of Juan Vicente Gómez, which takes us back to 1908. Everything has basically remained the same; it's been the same system of domination, with a different face – whether it's that of General Gómez or of Doctor Rafael Caldera. Behind this figure, this caudillo, with a military beret or without it, on horseback or in a Cadillac or a Mercedes Benz, it's been the same system – in economics and in politics – and the same denial of basic human rights and of the right of the people to determine their own destiny.

Chávez and his friends, from their position in the military academy, were well placed to recruit other young and discontented officers to their cause. In March 1985, they were joined by Major Francisco Javier Arias Cárdenas, a former pupil at a Catholic seminary who had returned from a postgraduate course in Colombia. Arias Cárdenas came from Zulia, and was destined to play an important role in the coup attempt that was eventually made in February 1992. He had many friends in the civilian left and, later in the 1990s, he was to join one of the smaller radical parties, La Causa R, and was elected as governor of his home state. He is often considered to be the most prominent intellectual within the Chávez movement, though he lacks Chávez's authority and charismatic charm.

Encouraged by Chávez, the participants in his Bolivarian Movement sought historical endorsement for their project in the ideas of three significant figures, known, although not well, to every Venezuelan school-child: Ezequiel Zamora, the *llanos* leader with whom Chávez had been familiar since childhood; Simón Bolívar, the Liberator; and Simón Rodriguez, often remembered as Bolívar's tutor though a man with an infinitely more interesting career than that simple fact would suggest.

From the start, the conspirators had a left-wing slant to their project. Soon they were using the language of the civilian left that some of them acquired when studying at the Universidad Central in Caracas. A unique characteristic of the Venezuelan military in the 1980s was that junior officers were sent to study social sciences in civilian universities. As they moved about in civil society, many young officers found themselves making contacts with the survivors of the guerrilla movements of the 1960s.

As the revolutionary officers made their way slowly up the military hierarchy, they began to consider when they might be in a position to stage a revolutionary coup. The year 1992 looked the earliest and most suitable moment, since that was when they might expect to be given command of troops. In the meantime, they became known as the Macate organization, short for 'Mayores, Capitanes and Tenientes', and later Comacate, adding 'Comandantes' to the earlier ranks.

It would have been difficult to keep such an organization secret, and military intelligence, the Dirección de Inteligencia Militar (the DIM), eventually got wind of their activities. The DIM knew about the radical lectures being given in the military academy, but they did not know what kind of conspiracy was afoot, or how widespread it had become. They knew that they were dealing with some of the most competent, popular and promotable young officers in the army, and to discipline them, or to sack them, would have caused serious disaffection within the ranks.

Hugo Chávez was clearly identified as a dangerous subversive, and the initial solution was to transfer him as far away from Caracas as possible. He was removed from his influential position in the military academy in 1986, and transferred to Elorza in the state of Apure, a distant point on the frontier close to Colombia.

I travelled to Elorza on a small local bus, a 12-hour journey from Barinas. The road is appalling, with a metalled surface that has long disintegrated. Elorza lies almost due south of Barinas, and the road crosses two of the great tributaries of the Orinoco, the Apure and the Arauca. A bridge over the Apure links Ciudad de Nutrias with Bruzual, and one day President Chávez plans to make these remote villages the heart of a great new development plan for the *llanos*.

Elorza lies even further south, on the far side of the Arauca river, over another fine bridge. A hotel, a main street, and a military base outside the town, this is rural Venezuela. The shops are run by

Syrians, the restaurants by Colombians, and a mixed group of indigenous people – Cuivas and Yaruros – live on the outskirts of the village. The mighty Arauca thunders past the northern edge of the village. I settled down to a meal of beef and yucca, and talked to the restaurant owner who was a refugee from the violence in Colombia, a few miles away across the border. He had moved here from Tolima, and found Venezuela relatively peaceful compared with the horrors of Colombia.

Chávez is remembered by people here with great affection, for he put their village on the map. He commanded a motorized division at the base down the road but used his years here to try out some of the ideas that now inform his political and social programme for the country. He encouraged experimental schemes of cooperation between soldiers and civilians, and soon the radical lieutenant at Elorza had become hugely popular throughout the whole region of Apure. As well as providing military support for social and economic development in the region, he widened the focus of his activities. Soon he was moving into the life of the community, organizing historical pageants and encouraging the collection of oral history records.

Somone must have forgotten his record or lost his file, for in 1988, in the final months of the presidency of another Acción Democrática politician, Jaime Lusinchi, Chávez was brought back to Caracas – to the presidential palace at Miraflores. Here he was given work as an aide to the national security council. Finally he was on his way up. He was sent on a visit to Central America that year, then at the height of the contra war in Nicaragua and the counter-insurgency campaigns in Guatemala.

In Elorza, Chávez had been isolated from his brother revolutionaries in the army. Once back in Caracas, he was better placed to continue the conspiratorial planning of his Bolivarian Revolutionary Movement. It was not before time, because the following year, in February 1989, the city of Caracas was to explode in an unexpected and unorganized rebellion. Chávez had always been hoping that something would 'turn up', yet when it did so the conspirators were not remotely prepared.

3

FEBRUARY 1989 (1):
THE REBELLION IN CARACAS,
THE CARACAZO

I immediately gathered my troops together and said: 'Hands up those who belong to the Country Club!' I looked at their expressions of surprise, and saw that they all remained motionless and silent . . . Then I said, well that means that we all must come from the shanty towns . . . like this one. The people who live here are like us, they are the people, our brothers; that means that no one must fire without authorization; no one must shoot unless we are attacked.

Major Francisco Arias Cárdenas, February 1989

Guarenas is a soulless satellite town some 30 kilometres east of Caracas where thousands of the capital's service workers have established their homes. The first signs of trouble began early on the Monday morning – 27 February 1989. People travelling in to the city by bus discovered that the fares had doubled that morning, and they began spontaneously to protest. Trouble soon flared in Petare, further in, and by mid-morning it had spread, via television, to the major cities of the country: Maracay, Valencia, Barquisimeto, Ciudad Guayana and Mérida.

Buses were overturned and burnt, but this was just the initial stage of the revolt. Within hours the rebellion had become more generalized, with widespread looting and the destruction of shops and supermarkets. Gangs of young people from the suburbs, both poor and angry, invaded the commercial centre of Caracas and moved on to the privileged residential areas of the wealthy under the slopes of Mount Avila, close to the heart of the city. Rioting and looting continued unchecked throughout the night and the following day. It developed into a prolonged and mighty rebellion – the *Caracazo* as it was called – but it was soon to be followed by days of brutal military repression.

Lieutenant Chávez was lying in bed that Monday morning with a contagious illness; indeed, the doctor at the Miraflores Palace had told him to go home lest he risk infecting the entire presidential household. During all their years of plotting, the young officers of the Bolivarian Revolutionary Movement had often discussed the possibility of a popular uprising that they might be able to turn to their advantage. Yet when it actually happened, they were totally unprepared, and some found themselves obliged to participate in the repression.

The impact of this urban revolt, both on the general population and on the soldiers involved, was to have a dramatic effect on the political developments of the subsequent decade. Indeed the contemporary history of Venezuela begins with this cardinal event, for it persuaded the Bolivarian officers to accelerate their plans.

The year 1989 was an important date for most of the rest of the world as well. The fall of the Berlin Wall in the autumn, and the subsequent collapse of the pro-Soviet governments in Eastern Europe, was quickly perceived as the harbinger of the end of the entire Communist era. In the same way, the *Caracazo*, which took place earlier in the year, marked the beginning of the end of Venezuela's *ancien régime*. The people had taken to the streets just 30 years earlier, in January 1958, and had paved the way, under the direction of the Patriotic Junta, for the overthrow of the dictatorship of General Pérez Jiménez. Now they were doing it again, almost by accident, to indicate their desire to get rid of their corrupt and bureaucratic government with its democratic façade. Yet whereas the uprising in 1958 had been organized, purposeful and politically inspired, the *Caracazo* of 1989 was anarchic, chaotic and leaderless.

It was such a spontaneous affair that it took the government's intelligence operations entirely by surprise. The efforts of the militarized secret police, the Disip, had been devoted for many years to infiltrating the political groups of the ultra-left, yet such groups had all but disappeared by the end of the 1980s, and they played no role in promoting the *Caracazo*. The Disip had never troubled itself to monitor the capacity for autonomous rebellion brewing in the *ranchos*, or shanty towns, of the suburban areas of the city. Military intelligence (the DIM) was by all accounts better informed. It knew that something was up and had warned the government that the Monday might well be a difficult day. Yet its warnings either failed to get through to the Miraflores Palace or were simply ignored.

'There were riots in the suburb of Guarenas on the first day,' says Heinz Sonntag, a sociology professor at the Centro de Estudios de Desarrollo in Caracas, who made a study of the *Caracazo*, 'and the police didn't intervene. They didn't do so on the following day either. The National Guard was then ordered in, but they refused to enter the *ranchos*. The government turned to the military.'

Soldiers now moved into the shanty towns, and cordoned off the high-rise state housing blocks (the creation, ironically, of the Pérez Jiménez era in the 1950s). They shot anything that moved. 'The official figure of those killed was 372, but the more probable figure is over two thousand – in Caracas alone.' Thousands were wounded. Sonntag believes that 'the repression was meant as "a warning" to the poor, so that they wouldn't do it again'. It worked for a long time, he says. 'People grew afraid.' The event cast a long shadow over the 1990s, creating a climate of hopelessness and political apathy that only began to be dispelled by the election of Chávez in 1998.

President Carlos Andrés Pérez had taken office at the beginning of February. This was his second term, and he knew the ropes – he had been president before, in the 1970s – but he was unprepared for this popular explosion. Holding a meeting of his council of ministers at midday on Tuesday 28 February, he decreed a state of emergency, a constitutional device that involved the suspension of all civil liberties. The army imposed a night-time curfew.

The immediate cause of the rebellion was the rise in the price of petrol, part of the new, neo-liberal economic 'packet' that Pérez had announced ten days earlier on 16 February. The petrol price had been scheduled to increase by 100 per cent on Sunday 26 February, but precisely in order to avoid the trouble that suddenly blew up in its face, the government had envisaged a staggered increase in bus fares. Bus owners were to be allowed to put up fares by 30 per cent on the first working day after the petrol price increase, the fateful Monday, while a further 30 per cent increase would be permitted three months later.

Many bus owners, of course, passed on the increase to their passengers on the very first day, putting up the fares by 100 per cent to cover their own increased costs. This was the cause of the inevitable eruption of anger among impoverished commuters, customarily short of money at the end of the month. A particular burden fell on students whose normal half-price concessions were withdrawn.

Within a few days, the terrified and terrorized inhabitants of the city had returned to some kind of normality. The poorer parts of the capital nursed their wounded and nourished a terrible grievance against the regime, while hundreds of bodies were buried in unmarked graves. The richer parts reinforced their steel fences and their security arrangements, and congratulated themselves on a lucky escape.

Yet in the long run the most significant impact of the *Caracazo* was on the armed forces charged with the repression. While some of the soldiers involved in shooting down their fellow citizens undoubtedly felt guilty and ashamed at the actions they had been ordered to take, the group of politically motivated officers associated with Chávez and the Bolivarian Revolutionary Movement felt aggrieved that the moment and the opportunity they had been half expecting had passed them by without any possibility of taking action. Their contacts with civilian groups outside, including some of the left-wing parties and some of the survivors of the guerrilla groups of the 1960s, had provided them with no warning of what was about to happen.

Many of the principal military conspirators were in Caracas during the *Caracazo*, but they all suffered different fates. Chávez himself was out of action, in bed, but two of his close associates, Francisco Arias Cárdenas and Felípe Acosta Carles, were ordered out into the *ranchos* to take part in the repression. In an unexplained incident, Acosta was shot dead. Some people, including Chávez, believe that the secret police, the Disip, were aware of his participation in the military conspiracy, in which case it is possible that he was killed by them rather than by the rioters. The same people think that Chávez was lucky to have been at home that week.

Arias Cárdenas was among those sent out to repress the rebellion. Later, in an interview with Angela Zago, he revealed his intense feelings of rage that the revolutionary movement in which he was involved had not been ready 'to stand side by side with the people in a civilian–military rebellion'. He felt that the army was on the wrong side in this war, and he made herculean efforts to try to ensure that his soldiers did not fire on the crowds. He was appalled by what he saw:

As soon as I arrived at the place that was to be my centre of operations, I realized that the officer from whom I had taken over had already been firing against the tower blocks, in an absolutely irresponsible and inhuman fashion. I also heard stories of the excesses committed by the political police, the Disip.

I immediately gathered my troops together and said: 'Hands up those who belong to the Country Club!' I looked at their expressions of surprise, and saw that they all remained motionless and silent. I repeated my request: 'Hands up those who live in Alto Prado, in Lagunita Country Club, or in Altamira!' [the wealthiest and most exclusive suburbs] Nobody moved.

Then I said, well that means that we all come from the shanty towns and the poor parishes like this one. The people who live here are like us, they are the people, our brothers; that means that no one must fire without authorization; no one must shoot unless we are attacked.

Some weeks later, Chávez returned to his duties in the presidential palace at Miraflores. On his way in, he was stopped by the palace guards, who, though not part of his conspiracy, were aware that something was in the wind. 'Look here, major,' one of them asked him, 'is it true about the Bolivarian Movement? We'd like to hear more about it; we're not prepared to go on killing people.' These were soldiers from the presidential guard, Chávez recalled, people trusted by the government. The conspiracy was clearly gathering pace, and the moment for decisive action could not be long postponed.

Yet the authorities were now on his track. At the end of the year, on 6 December 1989, the day on which new state governors were to be elected, Chávez and a number of army majors of his seniority were summoned to appear before the army high command. They were accused of plotting against the government, and of planning to assassinate the president and senior officers on Christmas Day. The information was false, and since nothing definite could be proved against them, the authorities could take no action. It was decided that they should be posted to different and distant places around the country. Chávez was given permission to enrol at the Simón Bolívar university in Caracas and began to work towards a master's degree in political science. Any coup attempt would have to be postponed.

Some eighteen months later, in August 1991, after taking a course at the staff college, Chávez was finally allocated a parachute battalion based at Maracay, to the west of Caracas. At last, with troops under his command, he was in a strong position to take the action for which he had so long prepared.

4

FEBRUARY 1989 (2):
THE ECONOMIC 'PACKET' THAT
DESTROYED THE PRESIDENCY
OF CARLOS ANDRÉS PÉREZ

The people's anguish is being expressed through demonstrations and protests, but we must understand that these are unavoidable. There was no other way out.

President Carlos Andrés Pérez, 1990

One afternoon in 1990, a year after the *Caracazo*, I went to see President Carlos Andrés Pérez in the little white, nineteenth-century building in the centre of Caracas that they call the Miraflores Palace. Pérez liked to meet foreign journalists and he was always extremely genial. I asked him how someone so closely involved with a specific form of statist economic development in the 1970s could have turned head over heels in the 1990s and embraced the economic doctrines of the International Monetary Fund that he had for so long opposed, especially since the fierce cuts he had imposed in 1989 had led directly to the *Caracazo*.

Pérez admitted that the *Caracazo* had been an unpleasant shock, and he agreed that his new policy had brought serious problems in its train. He also recognized that it had led to a rise in the cost of living:

The decisions I made were extremely difficult, and in general they are still quite unpopular. People resent the harsh measures we have taken. The people's anguish is being expressed through demonstrations and protests, but we must understand that these are unavoidable. There was no other way out . . . Times have changed quite a lot in these last fifteen years. The economy has become more global and better organized, and economic relations must be conceived differently. With this globalization of the economy, our people will understand better the need for foreign investment.

Venezuela was now in desperate need of such investment, the president said, since rent from oil was no longer sufficient to power the economy. He had even come to view oil refining, traditionally an area of exclusive investment by the state, as requiring 'the participation of foreign capital'.

Pérez was equally downcast about the future role of the state itself. Lessons had been learnt, he said, about the inherent nature of state institutions to degenerate. His government was planning to abolish 'all those elements where corruption would have been possible', though understandably he made no reference to his own role in the phenomenon. With a free exchange rate for the *bolívar*, and the abolition of licences for foreign trade operations, he hoped that corruption would simply wither away. 'The best thing for us,' he said, with the enthusiasm of a convert, 'is to reduce the intervention of the state to a minimum.'

Throughout the 1990s, much of the political rhetoric of Colonel Chávez was directed against 'neo-liberalism', against the programmes of economic reform imposed on Latin America in the 1990s by the government in Washington and so willingly accepted by Pérez. These programmes were made possible largely as a result of American control over financial agencies like the IMF and the World Bank, but also because Latin American economists and politicians, in significant numbers, had been successfully indoctrinated with the new American economic doctrines.

Although Chávez makes a general complaint against these programmes – he always refers to them as 'savage' neo-liberalism – his
particular arguments inevitably hark back to the dismal experience of
Venezuela during the years after 1989, and his chief target has been
the policy turnaround introduced by Pérez that had led directly to the
Caracazo, and was to lead later, in 1993, to the downfall of Pérez
himself.

The immediate cause of the Caracas rebellion, noted in the previous chapter, was the rise in the price of petrol, and therefore of bus
fares; this caused the Caracas commuters to rebel in the only way they
knew how. Yet the price rise was itself part of a more extensive change
in economic policy undertaken by the government earlier in the
month, swiftly dubbed *el gran viraje*, 'the great U-turn'.

The policies of neo-liberalism unleashed on Latin America (and
elsewhere) in the 1990s are often and usefully defined as the 'Washington Consensus', a ten-point programme originally devised and
codified in 1989 by John Williamson, formerly an IMF adviser in
the 1970s. The programme, deemed appropriate in Washington,
was directed essentially at countries with large foreign debts, forced
on them by international banks in the 1970s and 1980s. Its purpose
was to reform the internal economic mechanisms of debtor governments in Latin America (and elsewhere) so that they would be in a
position to repay the debts they had incurred, usually from American
banks.

Venezuela, with its large accumulation of debt, rashly borrowed
at high interest rates by a succession of corrupt and incompetent governments, was a prime target for the reforms of the 'Washington Consensus'. Some reform was clearly necessary if foreign investment was
to continue. Yet the specific reforms had a serious downside. While
taking into account the requirements of the foreign banks, they effectively ignored the needs of the poorer inhabitants of the debtor countries. In practice, of course, the reforms embraced a far wider agenda
than the mere solvency of a handful of international banks.

John Williamson, the codifier of the 'Washington Consensus',
explained his terms at a conference on the subject in 1994. He claimed

to have identified 'ten areas where policy-makers and scholars in "Washington" could arguably muster a fairly wide consensus as to the character of the policy reforms that debtor countries should pursue'.

Couched in the cool language of imperial economists, his programme might seem innocuous enough. Yet, in practice, the terms demanded of the debtor countries spelt out a new form of colonialism. The advantages granted to US-based transnational companies under the neo-liberal programme went far beyond a simple policy of debt recovery.

The 'ten areas' of the 'Washington Consensus', defined by Williamson, involved government agreeing to enforce the following reforms:

1. a guarantee of fiscal discipline, and a curb to budget deficits;
2. reduction in public expenditure, particularly in the military and in public administration;
3. tax reform, aiming at the creation of a system with a broad base and with effective enforcement;
4. financial liberation, with interest rates determined by the market;
5. competitive exchange rates, to assist export-led growth;
6. trade liberalization, coupled with the abolition of import licensing and a reduction in tariffs;
7. promotion of foreign direct investment;
8. privatization of state enterprises, leading to efficient management and improved performance;
9. deregulation of the economy;
10. protection of property rights.

This was the programme of economic reform that the Pérez government felt called upon to adopt in February 1989. An ideological blank page himself, the President accepted the prevailing wisdom without a qualm. Surrounding himself with a youthful crowd of young US-trained economists, versed in the disciplines of the Chicago School, he announced his new economic 'packet' two weeks after the official inauguration ceremonies.

To the two principal figures in his government responsible for the reform programme, the terms of the 'Washington Consensus' were meat and drink. Moisés Naím, the development minister, and Miguel Rodríguez, the minister of planning, were young whizz-kids from MIT and Yale. They were cut from the same cloth as Vaclav Klaus in Czechoslovakia and Lescek Balcerowicz in Poland, the economists who were to spearhead the free-market drive into Eastern Europe in the 1990s.

These men had all drunk deeply at the wells of neo-liberalism, and all shared a familiarity with the world of academic think-tanks, university lecture halls and international financial institutions. These were the shock troops of the new economic fundamentalism. Yet at the same time, they had an Achilles' heel. They suffered from a marked lack of knowledge or understanding of the political sphere in their own countries. The economics was self-evident, they thought; the politics could take care of itself.

During the last months of the regime of President Jaime Lusinchi, which had lasted from 1984 to 1989, everyone in Caracas had been aware of a looming economic crisis. This came to a head in January 1989, and Lusinchi's last act as president was to suspend repayment of the foreign debt. After twenty years of profligate spending and unparalleled corruption, the foreign reserves were about to run out. In the aftermath of that decision, people speculated about the policies the new Pérez government would be likely to promote when he took over in February. Pérez was remembered as the man in charge during the palmy days of 'Venezuela Saudíta' in the 1970s, when the country had appeared to be impossibly rich. The population had voted for his return to the presidential palace, largely in the improbable belief that he might work his magic a second time.

Pérez kept the country waiting. As president-elect, he spent some weeks visiting the principal countries of Opec – Saudi Arabia, Kuwait, and Algeria – suggesting perhaps that he planned to revive Venezuela's participation in the international politics of oil. When finally he returned to Caracas, his mind had been made up. He had decided, to most people's surprise, to embrace the revolutionary neo-liberal policies of the hour, which had not yet grown at that time into the new orthodoxy of the 1990s. Quite possibly, he could see no other way forward.

There would be a drastic revision in the role and the size of the old Venezuelan state, which had been such a dominant participant in the economics and politics of the previous half century. State enterprises would be privatized. The government would no longer seek to generate employment and economic growth through its own drive and impetus but through 'the accelerated expansion of the private sector'. It would also 'liberalize' prices and interest rates, and abolish the variable exchange rates.

Miguel Rodríguez, the planning minister, was the principal author of this programme of structural change. Some years later, when out of office, he proudly outlined what it had consisted of. He had fulfilled the terms of the 'Washington Consensus' down to the last dot and comma, producing a programme that went entirely contrary to everything that most Venezuelans had long believed in and held most dear:

> The programme was comprehensive in its design. It included complete trade reform, elimination of all trade restrictions, and reduction of tariffs to a narrow band; elimination of all exchange controls and adoption of a free float that would permit an exchange rate compatible with the development of non-traditional exports; price liberalization; the restructuring of the public sector with widespread decentralization and privatization of parastatal enterprises; a comprehensive tax reform; a new policy to set public sector prices at efficient levels; the restructuring of the financial sector, featuring liberalization, increased competition, and strengthening of the regulatory framework; modernization of labour legislation, including the creation of pension funds and the restructuring of the social security system; elimination of restrictions to foreign investment; restructuring of the external debt; an overhaul of the policy of external financing; and a new social policy that would eliminate the system of massive

generalized subsidies (many of which went to the rich) in favour of targeted subsidies directed to the poorest segment of the population.

This was the new economic strategy unleashed on Venezuela in February 1989, and, to crown it, President Pérez announced with some satisfaction and relief that his economic team had secured something from Washington in exchange: a loan from the International Monetary Fund for US$4,500 million dollars, to be made available over a period of three years. In earlier and happier times, when claiming leadership of the Third World in the 1970s, Pérez had denounced the economists of the IMF as 'genocide workers in the pay of economic totalitarianism'. Now he was having to go on all fours to beg for money from an institution he had once described as 'an economic neutron bomb' that 'killed people but left buildings standing'.

The *Caracazo* served to slow down his ambitious plans. In the first year, not a single state enterprise had been privatized. Pérez signed a decree favouring privatization in August 1989, but the Congress was unable to agree on the definition of the 'basic and strategic enterprises' that were to remain in the public sector. Many Congressmen were happy to drag their feet, but the time lost was not used by Pérez to prepare the country for the changes to come. For by 1990 it was clear that, whatever the temporary and peculiar hiccups of the process, Venezuela was now participating fully in the global revolution in economic thinking. The recipe was the same as in Prague or Warsaw, although the local conditions might be rather different.

When I interviewed Miguel Rodríguez that year, I found the minister sitting in his shirt sleeves under the statutory portrait of Bolívar and talking into two phones at once. Young economists may lack political experience but Rodríguez was clearly enjoying the exercise of power, relishing his intellectual superiority and his capacity not to suffer fools gladly.

He thought it was unfortunate that the country had grown accustomed to cheap oil and cheap electricity, 'sold to the consumer far below cost'. His adjustment programme, he said, was 'going to achieve efficient pricing in the public sector in a very short period of time'. He believed – with the elegant disdain of a technocrat – that the time had come to be tough. When I murmured something about the *Caracazo*, he dismissed it with a wave of the hand: 'It's not the man in the street who complains about an increase in petrol prices, it's the politicians, and two or three agitators in the universities and the high schools. The people understand these things.'

His main concern was the slow speed with which the government was getting its programme through the Congress. Delay deprived the government of the initiative, he said, allowing the opposition to regroup, and inertia to set in. He knew that both he and Naím were unpopular with the ruling bosses of Acción Democrática, and the lack of political support for their programme from the governing party was a serious drag on the impetus for economic reform. The Young Turks wanted to move quickly; the bosses urged caution.

In the long run, their lack of political understanding created the conditions for a military coup, and caused the downfall of their president. The political crisis that resulted from their economic programme had two outcomes that no one had remotely envisaged at the outset.

Spurred on by the horror of the *Caracazo*, Colonel Chávez redoubled his efforts to prepare his Bolivarian Revolutionary Movement for action, and in February 1992 he set out to do what the Acción Democrática bosses were able to perform a year later: to overthrow the president.

Chávez was unsuccessful, but the following year, before Pérez's term as president had run its course, the party bosses had resolved to get rid of him and throw him to the wolves. In 1993, Pérez was impeached by Congress on charges of corruption, placed under house arrest, and removed from office.

In February 1996, when he was still under house arrest, I went to talk to him again. He had lost the trappings of office, but in his mountain eyrie above El Hatillo outside Caracas he still gave the impression of a man awaiting the call of a people clamouring for his return.

'Venezuela is suffering from a tremendous structural crisis,' he said, from the far side of his huge desk. 'One of the reasons for the crisis is that the parties are in crisis – they have been for some time. In Copei, the structure of the party was in the hands of a man – Rafael Caldera – who wouldn't allow anyone to be a candidate for the presidency except himself.'

Pérez was equally critical of his own party, Acción Democrática, 'a party, unfortunately, that has been gobbled up by clientelism and the party machine. I was excluded from it, but I continue to have the support of the people who vote for it. Indeed that's why I'm imprisoned here, to keep me isolated, so that I don't have access to my political base. These limitations on my activity are serious, for I cannot hope to have a direct influence on what's going on.'

Pérez was right about Venezuela being in a state of crisis. What he was unable to recognize was that he was the man largely responsible for what had happened. The people were not clamouring for his return, but for his head – and in February 1992 he had nearly lost it.

5

DOUGLAS BRAVO AND THE
DEBATE BETWEEN SOLDIERS
AND CIVILIANS

> Chávez did not want civilians to participate as a concrete force.
> He wanted civil society to applaud but not to participate . . .
>
> Douglas Bravo, interviewed in 1999

The road from Barinas to Mérida is one of the great scenic routes of Latin America, winding up from the heat of the Orinoco plains to the limpid atmosphere of the Andean valleys, while zig-zagging through forests and avoiding waterfalls. I found a 'por puesto' in the Barinas bus station, and waited for it to fill up. The 'por puesto' is a taxi or small bus that only leaves when its complement of seats is entirely taken up. Not long after our eventual departure, the engine of the minibus phuttered to a stop, and nothing the driver could do would persuade it to revive. We all got out and stood around in the road for an hour or so before another minibus arrived to rescue us, and to take us on and up, through the clouds and over the mountain pass to Mérida.

Mérida is an alpine town, spread along a broad valley and surrounded by green mountains. Not much remains of the old colonial structure, but it still retains the charm of a small university town, where the youthful student population crowds the streets in the mornings and evenings and through the lunch hour. This is the intellectual heartland of Venezuela, an oasis of peace and calm after the urban nightmare of Caracas. People come here on holiday to refresh their batteries, and the professors here at the Universidad de los Andes usually stay put, regarding Caracas as Babylon.

Mérida has always been a leftist centre, and after the collapse of the guerrilla movements of the 1960s many former guerrillas came to live in and around the town. While some of the guerrilla survivors had regrouped in the 1970s in the Movimiento al Socialismo, others had joined the Partido de la Revolución Venezolano (PRV), an organization set up by Douglas Bravo, the guerrilla leader in Falcón state, after his break with the Communist Party in 1966. The PRV was a legal political organization, and one of its supporters at the university in Mérida was Adán Chávez, the colonel's elder brother, and a professor in the science faculty. In the early 1980s, Adán Chávez perceived that it would be useful to organize a meeting between Bravo, his revolutionary friend, and Hugo, his revolutionary brother.

Douglas Bravo recalls the meeting, which seems to have taken place in 1982 or 1983. 'The movement involved in these initial discussions with Chávez was the PRV.' Bravo says that he talked with Chávez and 'with other officers' who had been participating 'in the revolutionary structure we were preparing'. Their purpose was to construct 'a civilian–military movement, with the long-term aim of preparing a revolutionary insurgency'.

Recently, in an interview with Alberto Garrido, Bravo has given a fairly full account of what was being considered. 'We did not envisage an immediate uprising, we were all clear about that, both the military and the civilians . . .' Both sides agreed that unless there was a significant political development in the country – 'a sense of expectation in the mass of the people' – nothing much would happen until the military conspirators were senior enough to have command of troops.

As it happened, the *Caracazo* of February 1989 proved to be the 'significant development' among the mass of the people that they had been half expecting, although neither the civilians nor the military were prepared for it.

Throughout the political and economic crisis of the 1980s, a number of civilian and military groups had been circling around each other, making spasmodic contact. A wide spectrum of civilian groups hostile to Venezuela's corrupt and inadequate political system were happy to make contact with subversive officers in the armed forces.

The Bolivarian Revolutionary Movement of Colonel Chávez was by no means the only politicized grouping within the armed forces at that time. There was a subversive cell in the navy, about which little is publicly known, but it was not connected with the group led by Admiral Hernán Grüber that organized the second coup in 1992. There was also a group in the air force, developed by Lieutenant William Izarra, a revolutionary officer with Trotskyist leanings who had studied at Harvard.

In the early 1980s, at a time when Chávez was organizing his Bolivarian Movement in the army, Izarra had formed a revolutionary cell in the air force and called it the Alianza Revolucionaria de Militares Activos (ARMA), the Revolutionary Alliance of Active Service Officers. Like Chávez he held meetings with civilian politicians, with Teodoro Petkoff of the Movimiento al Socialismo (MAS), and with José Vicente Rangel. Both had been presidential candidates of the more-or-less united left, though nothing concrete emerged from their discussions with Izarra.

Izarra was later to join up with Chávez after the 1992 coup, and was put in charge of the international relations of Chávez's political party, the Fifth Republic Movement. In November 1998, he was elected as a senator. After disagreements with Luís Miquilena in December 1998, he eventually parted company with Chávez, resigning his seat in the Senate in May 1999 to set up his own party, the Movimiento de Democracia Directa.

Chávez seems always to have been convinced of the need for civilians to be involved in his project. He had been influenced in the 1970s by the military revolution in Peru, and he well understood from his reading of its history that the eventual failure of General Velasco's government was due to its lack of civilian participation, which had led in turn to a lack of popular support. Both Chávez and Admiral Grüber believed that civilian support was necessary for the eventual success of their 'military interventions' and that well-selected civilian political groups should be involved from the start.

Chávez had not limited his discussions with civilian revolutionaries to Douglas Bravo's group. He had also established a relationship at an early stage with the political leaders of La Causa R, the Radical Cause, a leftist organization active in Caracas and Bolívar state, and had met its founder, Alfredo Maneiro, shortly before his death in November 1982. Maneiro was another of the charismatic revolutionaries to have emerged from the guerrilla struggle of the 1960s.

The supporters of La Causa R were among those who might have cooperated with a military rebellion, and Chávez had an idea how they might be used. He had been intrigued by the organization set in place by the left-wing military government of General Omar Torríjos in Panama. Torríjos, and subsequently Manuel Noriega, had organized a kind of civilian paramilitary grouping, known as the 'Dignity Battalion', capable of acting in support of the military.

Chávez had seen this battalion undergoing training in Panama, and had been impressed by its apparent capacity to act as an irregular unit, blocking roads and performing other tasks, in association with more regular insurrectionary forces. He approached the leaders of La Causa R with this project:

> We made suggestions over the years to these people that they should form 'dignity battalions', made up of civilians from the shanty towns, and led by genuine community leaders. We provided material about different weapons, and we gave classes in the use of arms, though we couldn't provide them with arms for obvious reasons. We were under permanent surveillance.

Nothing much developed from these embryonic contacts that Chávez made with La Causa R, and they seem to have left him with doubts about their capacity to deliver. Chávez feared that some leftist groups were simply hoping that a tactical alliance with the military would help to hoist them into power, while he perceived that others were unhappy, in their heart of hearts, about the idea of relying on military men to prosecute the revolution.

Any discussion between civilian leftists and potentially revolutionary officers was bound to raise disruptive questions. More important than the issue of what role civilians might play in the unfolding of a military coup was the question of the kind of participation they might expect to have in a subsequent government. This was not an academic argument. Much of the left in Venezuela had felt historically betrayed by what had happened after the civilian–military uprising organized by the Patriotic Front of 1958. The people then had been badly deceived. Many had subsequently taken part in the guerrilla war of the 1960s in a bid to recover what they believed they had been cheated of.

After the *Caracazo*, Douglas Bravo resumed contact with Chávez, though Bravo claims that Chávez soon began to detach himself from 'the revolutionary elements' with whom he was in contact. After several disagreements, the last meeting between the two men took place in October 1991, four months before the coup that Chávez was to make in February 1992. They tried to iron out their differences. According to Bravo's account:

> We met to talk about the plans for the uprising . . . We said that first of all there should be a civil action, like the general strike organized by the Patriotic Junta on January 23 [1958]. The military action would come later. This was so that civil society should have an active participation in the revolutionary movement. But that was exactly what Chávez did not want. Absolutely not! Chávez did not want civilians to participate as a concrete force. He wanted civil society to applaud but not to participate, which is something quite different . . .

Bravo recounts one rather damaging story of an incident in that period:

Some 20 or 25 guerrillas were assembled, and Chávez brought his action plan for a military coup. The coup bore no resemblance to the idea we had previously discussed with him that the civilian population should take an active part . . . As a result, when he announced his plan, one of those present at the meeting said: 'José María [his undercover name] I can see all the military units that will be mobilized, from Maracaibo, from Valencia, from Carora, from Barquisimeto, from Yaracuy, from Maracay, from Caracas, but where are the rest of us, the civilians, where do we fit in to this plan?' Chávez replied firmly: 'Civilians get in the way. We shall summon them when we get into power.'

Bravo argues that this was not just a tactic on Chávez's part: 'It was his political position.'

Breaking off relations with Bravo, Chávez continued to hold meetings with other old revolutionaries from the PRV, notably with Kléber Ramírez, a former guerrilla who had become an adviser to Colonel Arias Cárdenas. Both men had been educated in a Catholic seminary and had much in common. Ramírez was involved in the preparations for the coup of February 1992, but was eventually blamed, probably unfairly, for unwittingly betraying the earlier plan to stage the coup in December 1991.

One problem associated with the strategy of permitting civilian involvement in a military coup, though not perceived by Chávez in the early stages, was that civilian revolutionaries rarely had the kind of hermetic discipline associated with military conspiracies. The greater the involvement of civilians in the plans of the Bolivarian Movement, the greater the risk of discovery.

Chávez eventually became disillusioned with many of the old leftists, and they with him. Later he reflected on the adverse impact that the guerrilla strategy of the 1960s had had on the country's political development:

One of the unfortunate effects of the guerrilla war in Venezuela was the isolation of political leaders who might otherwise have contributed to the development of a different mentality and outlook in the country. Many of them remained in the mountains, or jumped into the opposite camp. I think that this isolated and cut off an entire generation that might have created new political currents.

There has been a huge leadership vacuum – in the workers' movement, among the peasants, in the shanty towns, and in the whole of society. Given this historical situation, we have to dedicate ourselves to transforming the collective consciousness through action. We have to fill the vacuum, summoning up a new leadership . . .

This analysis, with its all too accurate description of much of the Venezuelan left, was not dissimilar from that of Alfredo Maneiro and La Causa R. While Chávez did not secure much action or support from the old guerrilla leadership, it was certainly to influence his thinking.

6

4 FEBRUARY 1992: THE 'MILITARY INTERVENTION' OF CHÁVEZ

Comrades: unfortunately, for the moment, the objectives that we had set ourselves have not been achieved in the capital . . . those of us here in Caracas have not been able to seize power.

Colonel Hugo Chávez, 4 February 1992

In the early hours of the morning of Tuesday 4 February 1992, five army units led by Colonel Chávez moved by road into Caracas. Chávez at this time was the commander of a parachute regiment based at Maracay, some 50 miles from the capital. The principal aim of the insurgents was to detain President Carlos Andrés Pérez and arrest the entire high command of the armed forces. Orders were then to have gone out to garrison commanders throughout the country to obey the edicts of the new government.

One unit attacked the defence ministry, another advanced on La Carlota, the military airport inside the city, while a third moved towards the Miraflores Palace. Chávez himself drove to the Historical Museum, near the palace, where plans had been made to instal communications equipment. From there, he would direct the countrywide operation that he had unleashed.

President Pérez was out of the country, but contacts within the palace had informed the conspirators that he was scheduled to return that day, arriving at Maiquetía airport, close to the port of La Guaira. 'The idea was to detain Pérez at the airport,' Chávez later explained to Agustín Blanco Muñoz, 'and to take him, via the motorway, to the Historical Museum; our boys had organized a commando raid at the airport that would have captured him, but they were unable to enter, for it had been put under guard since midday.'

The conspiracy had in fact been betrayed the previous day, though the authorities were unaware of the details of the rebellion or of its dimensions. General Fernándo Ochoa Antich, the defence minister, knew that something was up, and had gone in person to meet President Pérez at Maiquetía, organizing a small force to be mobilized there from the National Guard and the marines.

'The second attempt,' Chávez continued, 'was to have been in the motorway tunnel, blocking the road with a burnt out car; but there were too many guards, and our forces were insufficient. Afterwards our plans included taking him at his house at La Casona, where there was a serious attack, but the forces of the Disip fought back. Pérez arrived there, but a few minutes before it was surrounded, he made off to the Miraflores Palace. When he got there, our tanks attacked, but he escaped through an unguarded entrance.'

Hugo Chávez and the principal conspirators of the Bolivarian Revolutionary Movement had always hoped that the year 1992 would be a suitable time to launch a coup d'etat. Chávez took over the parachute regiment in Maracay in August 1991; Jesús Urdaneta and Joel Acosta Chirinos received their regiments a week earlier. Francisco Arias Cárdenas, who worked in intelligence and had always managed to keep a low conspiratorial profile, had already been given an artillery regiment in Maracaibo the previous year.

Chávez realized that the military authorities were aware of some of his activities, though not of their extent. In December 1989, he and others had been hauled before an inquisition of senior generals who believed him to be organizing a coup, but he had escaped unscathed. But he knew that he needed to act swiftly. His initial plan was to stage a coup in December 1991, but the details appear to have been betrayed, possibly by his civilian collaborators.

In February 1992, the agreed strategy was to advance on Caracas and to capture the president and the senior generals. If the conspirators failed to detain the president, their insurrectionary movement would be stillborn. Chávez knew that about 10 per cent of the armed forces were firmly on his side. But if President Pérez was not captured in the first hours, and remained free to give orders to the 40 battalion commanders likely to remain loyal, the government would inevitably win. Chávez's own account runs as follows:

> We had been on the alert since Thursday January 30. A final meeting had been held on Sunday, at a petrol station on the Panamerican highway, with the Bolivarian conspirators in the air force, Francisco Visconti Osorio and Luís Reyes Reyes.
>
> I remember that on Sunday 2 February, almost at midnight, our people rang me from the Miraflores Palace and told me, in code, the date and time of the return of Pérez. That was the moment that we began to activate the operation, and on the Monday we woke up and started getting people on the move.

Chávez said goodbye to his wife and children, leaving her a cheque and money in cash that he had taken from his bank account in Maracay. By the evening of Monday 3 February, the conspirators were in control of the barracks at Maracay and Maracaibo, and a number of other cities, an essential preliminary to the advance on Caracas. But an exchange of telephone messages with other military bases, conducted in simple code, revealed that not all was well:

'I can't make it.'

'The party's today, send me the whisky.'

'No, we can't send the whisky, we couldn't get the money.'

'OK, don't send me anything.'

The conspirators did not realize at the time that they had already been betrayed. Earlier on the Monday, at midday, a captain in the military academy in Caracas, detailed by Chávez to seize its senior officers, decided to tell the director what was afoot. The military high command now knew they were faced with a coup attempt, but they did not know where it would come from. They had just 24 hours to find out, and to regain control of the country.

At 8 o'clock that evening, Chávez's column of soldiers, loaded into a fleet of hired buses, began to move on Caracas from Maracay. Chávez himself arrived at his designated position at the Historical Museum at 1 o'clock in the morning. He had hoped to direct operations from within the museum, but was greeted with a rude surprise. His troops came under machine-gun fire. For the first time he was forced to recognize that his plans had been betrayed. With some adroit arguing, he gained entry to the museum, persuading the colonel in charge that his men had come to reinforce the position. But when he got inside, he found that the communications equipment he was expecting to use had not been delivered. Out of touch with rebellious units in the rest of the country, he was now alone and isolated.

Elsewhere in the capital, a group of soldiers had attacked the presidential palace, but they proved unable to break through. The situation of the conspirators was now critical, and deteriorating. Reinforcements were blocked on the outskirts of Caracas, the air force generals in the conspiracy decided that it was too risky to allow their planes to take off, and a civilian group that was supposed to have seized the television and radio stations failed to do so. The conspirators were facing disaster.

In the aftermath of the coup, considerable debate arose within the ranks of the military conspirators about the role of the civilian supporters. In Valencia, it seems, civilians supporting the coup arrived at the barracks, and were indeed given weapons and vehicles, and they helped to seize the city. In Caracas and Maracaibo this did not happen. According to Chávez:

The civilians didn't show up. I had a lorry near Miraflores filled with guns to be handed out to the civilians. Although it's true that we didn't control the media, and were unable to appeal for popular support, it's also true that there were people who knew that that was the night of the operation, people who knew the password, 'Páez-Patria', to ask for weapons. But they didn't show up. We are not the only ones to blame. There were people who had known about the operation in advance, and they simply didn't come.

Early in the morning of 4 February, President Pérez appeared on television. He announced to a startled nation that a military rebellion had occurred in Maracay and was now in the process of being crushed. Watching the broadcast, Chávez realized that his coup had failed. At 9 o'clock, he decided to surrender.

At this stage something rather extraordinary occurred. To avoid further bloodshed, Chávez asked to be allowed to speak on television so that the colonels who had seized barracks and cities in other parts of the country might also peacefully surrender. Individual officers, like Francisco Arias Cárdenas in Maracaibo, were still in control of their regions, but since the plot had failed in Caracas, there was no chance of countrywide success.

Chávez's appearance on television lasted for just over a minute. Its unexpected result was to turn him from a wholly unknown colonel into a national figure. One minute of air time, at a moment of personal disaster, converted him into someone perceived as the country's potential saviour.

His broadcast was directed principally at the parachute regiment in Aragua and the tank brigade in Valencia. These two forces had successfully occupied their towns, and were showing no signs of wishing to surrender. Chávez realized that if they did not do so, there would be a bloodbath. He spoke confidently, and without notes:

First I want to say 'good morning' to all the people of Venezuela, but this Bolivarian message is directed specifically to the courageous soldiers of the parachute regiment of Aragua and the tank regiment of Valencia.   *por ahora*

Comrades: unfortunately, for the moment, the objectives that we had set ourselves have not been achieved in the capital. That's to say that those of us here in Caracas have not been able to seize power. Where you are, you have performed well, but now is the time for a rethink; new possibilities will arise again and the country will be able to move definitively towards a better future.

So listen to what I have to say, listen to comandante Chávez who is sending you this message, and, please, think deeply. Lay down your arms, for in truth the objectives that we set ourselves at a national level are not within our grasp.

Comrades, listen to this message of solidarity. I am grateful for your loyalty, for your courage, and for your selfless generosity; before the country and before you, I alone shoulder the responsibility for this Bolivarian military uprising. Thank you.

Two phrases from this short broadcast made a particular impact. No one in Venezuela had ever heard a politician apologize for anything before. In spite of the political and economic failures of recent years – the devaluation of the money, the bank collapses, the trials for corruption, the economic decline – no one in a position of power had ever said sorry, or accepted any portion of blame. And now here was a military officer saying he accepted responsibility for something that had gone wrong. This was something entirely new.

The other phrase that caught the popular imagination was 'for the moment', *por ahora*. The objectives of the rebellion had not been achieved 'for the moment', but this was read by most people optimistically, as a sign that Chávez would return to the struggle at some later date. His revolutionary project of overthrowing the government had been thwarted, but it would be revived. Chávez himself recalls that the words he uttered simply slipped out; he had no ulterior motive in saying *por ahora*. For years afterwards, it was to become his trademark, an implicit promise that he would return.

When the coup was over, with the leading conspirators safely behind bars, the politicians of the *ancien régime* returned to a country that had been dramatically changed: the monolithic institution of the armed forces was now seriously divided, and the great mass of the population was lining up solidly behind the coup leader.

Politicians had to adjust their discourse to this new reality. At an emergency session of the Congress, held immediately after the coup, former president Rafael Caldera made a powerful speech that came within an inch of endorsing it. His words were certainly read as such by the population. He was re-elected as president two years later, in December 1993, regarded by many people as the only significant political figure who had understood the mood of the country.

Caldera's speech firmly put the blame for trouble in the armed forces on the shoulders of President Pérez and on his neo-liberal economic programme. He uttered a number of home truths:

We must recognize – though it hurts to say so but it's the truth – that we have found no evidence in the popular classes, among the great bulk of non-political Venezuelans, of any enthusiasm, or any immediate and selfless decision, to take action that might have put a stop to this threat to constitutional order.

I must say to the President of the Republic, speaking from this tribune with a great sense of responsibility, that he has the principal responsibility to make the immediate changes that the country is demanding, though of course it depends on all of us as well.

It is difficult to ask people to sacrifice themselves in a struggle to defend liberty and democracy, when you know that democracy and the rule of law has not been able to provide them with food, or prevented exaggerated increases in the cost of living; it has not been able to put a stop to the terrible round of corruption that has eroded the institutional legality of the country, as everyone has seen with their own eyes. This is not something that can be hidden.

A military coup, whatever form it takes, must be censured and condemned; yet it would be naive to think that this was an event in which a handful of ambitious men threw themselves rashly into an adventure, on their account, without being aware of the wider implications of their action. There was a set of circumstances here, a backcloth to these developments, which is the serious situation in which the country finds itself. If this situation is not dealt with, the future may yet hold unpleasant surprises for us all.

Caldera was not quite alone in giving a speech that was read as a coded message of support for the coup. His speech was followed by one from Aristóbulo Istúriz, a former leader of the teachers' union and a Congressman from La Causa R. Like Caldera, Istúriz was rewarded for his outspoken views by the electorate. He was later elected as mayor of Caracas (and was subsequently the vice-president, supporting Chávez, of the Constituent Assembly in 1999).

Fourteen soldiers were killed during the coup, 50 were wounded, and some 80 civilians were wounded in the crossfire. More than 1,000 soldiers were subsequently detained.

For some months there was considerable debate about the role of the defence minister, General Fernándo Ochoa Antich. Chávez had certainly known him for many years, and there were many allegations that he had had something to do with the coup. These were never proved, but some people believed that he had moved rather slowly against officers known to be conspiring. In the incestuous world of the Venezuelan political elite, it was well known that his brother, Enrique Ochoa Antich, was on the left. Enrique was a prominent member, and later the secretary-general, of the Movimiento al Socialismo, the left-wing party that was to throw its weight behind Chávez's presidential campaign in 1998. A decent if bumbling man, General Ochoa was subsequently transferred from the defence ministry to become minister of foreign affairs, and was eventually banished to Mexico as ambassador. But in February 1992, it fell on his shoulders to enquire into the state of the armed forces. Why had there nearly been a successful coup? What could be done to prevent it happening again?

7

27 NOVEMBER 1992:
THE COUP BY ADMIRAL
HERNÁN GRÜBER

How is it possible that in the Soviet Union they could sack their defence minister and other high officials when a young German pilot landed his plane on Moscow's Red Square, while in Venezuela the army commander still keeps his job after half his forces have taken part in a rebellion, and everyone pretends that nothing has happened?

Admiral Hernán Grüber, March 1992

With Colonel Chávez behind bars after his 'military intervention' in February 1992, the second coup attempt later the same year seemed almost like a coda to the first, though it was considerably more violent. On 27 November, a further effort was made to capture President Pérez, and the Miraflores Palace was bombed from the air. Heavy fighting took place, both in Caracas and in Maracay, and more than 170 people were killed.

The chief organizer of the coup was Admiral Hernán Grüber Odremán from the navy, assisted by Francisco Visconti Osorio from the air force, a member of the Bolivarian conspiracy whose planes had failed to take off in February. Both officers were later to play a political role in the government of President Chávez in 1999, Grüber as the governor of Caracas, and Visconti as a member of the Consituent Assembly.

Admiral Grüber was not a natural rebel. Born in Upata on 17 February 1940, he came from a long-established German immigrant family, farming land in the state of Bolívar once owned by the missions of Caroní. He joined the navy in 1958, while his brother, Roberto, joined the army and eventually rose to be a general. Grüber took part in the suppression of the left-wing guerrillas in Lara and Anzoátegui in the 1960s, and subsequently was appointed to senior positions in frontier areas, notably on the Colombian border at Puerto Páez.

In the aftermath of the Chávez coup, considerable discussion took place, both within the government and within the armed forces, about what would happen next. What was behind the conspiracy? How far had it spread? And what measures could be taken to stop the rot?

In the middle of March 1992, some six weeks after the Chávez coup, General Ochoa, the defence minister, summoned Admiral Grüber for a private discussion. They were joined by another senior naval officer, Admiral Luís Enrique Cabrera Aguirre. At issue was the continuing groundswell of discontent within the military. One particular grievance, high on the agenda, was the way in which junior and low grade officers had been promoted to senior rank at the whim of civilian politicians, disregarding all established procedures.

A version of the meeting written up by Grüber was clearly designed to enlist sympathy for his cause. Yet it gives a chilling account of the extent of the dissatisfaction within the armed forces, and the outspoken way in which senior officers were prepared to voice their preoccupations to their indecisive political masters.

General Ochoa told the two admirals that he was concerned about the situation inside the armed forces. He perceived that it was 'still very delicate'. He had heard 'accounts of serious discontent among middle-ranking and junior officers', he said, and he wanted to know what the two admirals thought was going on.

'Look,' replied Admiral Cabrera, 'you must understand that the senior ranks have lost all credibility and trust. It's that simple. The subalterns no longer believe in their generals and colonels.'

'How can you be so certain?' asked Ochoa. 'Do you put them all in the same camp?'

'From generals and colonels who have all been promoted as a result of carrying the bags of some senator or other,' replied Cabrera, 'what can you expect.'

'So what should be done?' asked Ochoa, turning to Grüber.

'You want me to tell you?' Admiral Grüber replied pithily (and this of course is his own highly coloured account). 'The entire high command should be asked to resign. They should be retired immediately, and replaced by officers with genuine military qualifications.'

'But that would lead to chaos,' objected Ochoa.

'Look,' Grüber went on, 'the chaos will get worse as the military discontent accumulates. How is it possible that in the Soviet Union they could sack their defence minister and other high officials when a young German pilot landed his plane on Moscow's Red Square, while in Venezuela the army commander still keeps his job after half his forces have taken part in a rebellion, and everyone pretends that nothing has happened?'

It was a good question, but General Ochoa took no action. He could neither sack the high command, nor could he discipline the junior officers who were clearly plotting another coup. Like a rabbit caught in the headlights, the entire government was paralysed, unable to act.

Ochoa did manage to set in train the preparation of an academic survey of the situation within the armed forces. He wanted to get a clear overview of the dimensions of the dissent. Admiral Cabrera was handed this important task, and provided with a team of university researchers. They interviewed a large number of senior politicians and generals, both in retirement and in active service, and they also sent questionnaires to 5,000 servicemen stationed at the most important garrisons in the country – Aragua, Táchira, Zulia, Monagas and Caracas.

Their report, signed by Cabrera, was ready in the middle of July. It revealed the existence of five serious complaints about the condition of the armed forces and about the state of the nation, and made a number of comments and recommendations. Some of the complaints were about conditions of service: the inadequate nature of the health service within the armed forces; the ineffectiveness of the social security system; and the 'poor' perception of the system of promotions and of the provision of compensation for the loss of seniority. Other complaints indicated a more general (and thus less remediable) discontent: a lack of leadership; and the culture of corruption, both political and military, that permeated the country at the highest level.

The chief of the general staff, General Iván Jiménez Sánchez, received the report and took note of it. He even promised that he would set up a commission to ensure that its recommendations were implemented. Inevitably, perhaps, given the political stasis in the country, the report was shelved.

In August 1992, with no guarantee of any reforms in the wake of the February coup, and with no attention paid to the July report, Admiral Grüber's faction began to plot a new coup. Those included in his conspiracy were Cabrera from the navy, Visconti from the air force, and a number of civilian contacts, chiefly from La Causa R. Grüber's faction also enjoyed the support of the surviving members of Chávez's Bolivarian Revolutionary Movement, directed from Chávez's cell in the Yare prison. They called themselves the 'July 5 Movement', in homage to the independence struggle and Venezuela's national day.

More time seems to have been spent on planning events after the imagined success of their coup than on thinking how they might make the actual uprising more effective than the previous one. The initial political plan was to form a Council of State, comprising both civilians and officers, with a civilian as president, which would last for a year or so, and try to reorganize the country. The model was that of the Patriotic Junta of 1958, though they were also aware of the consequences of Rómulo Betancourt's coup against General Medina

Angarita on 18 October 1945, when a 'Revolutionary Junta' had been installed in the Miraflores Palace.

Their plans were subject to innumerable delays, and several key plotters seemed to lose enthusiasm as the weeks went by. Elections, for governors and mayors, were due in December, and the conspirators realized that their actions might be miscontrued if their coup were to occur during or after that event. They decided that they would have to act quickly, in November. Admiral Grüber, whose pseudonym was 'Julius Caesar', describes in his memoirs how the decision was taken 'to cross the Rubicon'.

On 25 November, he put the final touches to his preparations, making a video recording of the speech that he planned to have broadcast to the nation on the day of the coup. He practised before the cameras, and the technicians seemed satisfied with the result.

Two days later, on the morning of 27 November, he arrived at his headquarters to preside over what he hoped would be a well-organized coup. Yet as before, in the case of the Chávez coup, there were serious errors and omissions, with important participants failing to keep their promised appointments. Worst of all was the failure of the communications equipment. Like Chávez before him, Grüber had no means of keeping in touch with the officers in other parts of the country. He too was destined to be isolated and out of touch.

There was one difference. This time, the conspirators had managed to seize a television station, and Grüber pinned his hopes on a civilian uprising. If his video were to be shown on television screens across the nation, calling for support for his programme of national reconstruction, he fondly imagined that the masses would rise up and support his rebellion.

Disaster struck again, and no one seems to know quite how it happened. Instead of the measured and recorded tones of the admiral, announcing a coup d'etat and calling for popular support, a series of conflictive images flickered across the television screen. Masked men appeared, and promptly embarked on a round of looting reminiscent of the *Caracazo*; occasional bursts of rhetoric could be heard from the voice of the imprisoned Colonel Chávez.

It seems that the videos had been switched, or perhaps the operator had picked up the wrong one to put in his machine. No one subsequently claimed responsibility for what went wrong. The television-watching nation, preparing to go to work, did not know whether to laugh or cry. They certainly had no intention of going out into the streets to support a revolution organized in such an incompetent way.

Later in the morning, as he had done in February, President Pérez appeared on the screen to announce that all was well, and at midday Admiral Grüber surrendered. At that very moment, an air force plane passed over Caracas, making a supersonic bang. Grüber's video that was never shown had mentioned a fly-past, as the signal for the people to take to the streets. Now, nobody moved. Visconti wisely embarked his air-force conspirators onto a Hercules cargo plane, and set off across Colombia to seek sanctuary in Peru. At the prisons of Yare and San Carlos, a new group of failed military conspirators joined Colonel Chávez behind bars.

LUÍS MIQUILENA AND THE
PATRIOTIC FRONT OF 1989

A Patriotic Front cannot be invented; you cannot assemble a hundred distinguished figures and say 'We are the Front'. I don't believe in that.

Hugo Chávez interviewed in August 1995

Colonel Chávez and Admiral Grüber did not act alone. The planners of the two attempted coups in 1992 had both envisaged a revolutionary change in government that would be made by soldiers acting in alliance with civilian groups. They had looked essentially to the forces of the Venezuelan left, with its long tradition of encouraging, and participating in, military subversion. Most coup attempts in the previous half century, notably in 1944 (against Medina Angarita), in 1958 (against Pérez Jiménez) and in 1962 (against Rómulo Betancourt), had all taken place with the participation of civilians.

In the wake of the *Caracazo* of February 1989, a group of civilian activists anxious to take advantage of the popular explosion, had sought to renew this tradition. They came together to form a new 'Patriotic Front', a political device that crops up from time to time in Venezuelan history when people of goodwill across the spectrum get together to try to change the course of events during troubled times.

A 'Patriotic Front' had played an important role in the downfall of Pérez Jiménez in 1958, and in the more distant past a similar front was created in the 1850s, in the days of Ezequiel Zamora.

The Venezuelan elite has often liked to think of its country as 'a democracy', yet this has been a comparatively new development. Venezuela has been no stranger to military rule – it was run by military dictators during the first half of the twentieth century and for much of the nineteenth century as well. With such a history, it is hardly surprising that politicians should seek to involve the military in their plans, and the left has been no exception to this rule. 'Venezuelans are so accustomed to make the army the arbiter of their political contests,' wrote Rafael Caldera in the 1970s, 'that at any moment the most varied groups, for the most dissimilar ends, attempt to involve the army in new adventures to change our political reality.'

During the Second World War, the government of General Isaías Medina Angarita enjoyed the support of the Communist Party, and the military coup that overthrew this government in 1944 was organized by the civilian politicians of Acción Democrática, including Rómulo Betancourt, and, in a junior capacity, Carlos Andrés Pérez. Later, in 1958, the military government had been overthrown by the Patriotic Front of the time, a group within the left that conspired with sections of the military. The left had then given warm support to the presidential campaign of Admiral Wolfgang Larrazabal. Finally, in 1962, during the leftist guerrilla campaign against Betancourt's regime, civilian leftists were intimately involved in two important military revolts at Carúpano and Puerto Cabello.

The new Patriotic Front that assembled after the *Caracazo* in 1989 was presided over by Luís Miquilena, once the leader of the bus drivers' union in Caracas in the 1940s, and one of the great survivors of the Venezuelan left. He was eventually to become the chief political adviser of Colonel Chávez and, when over 80, the president of the Constituent Assembly in 1999.

The participants in the Front were all interested in the creation of a political alliance between civilians and the military, and much of the internal debate aroused in Venezuela since the advent of the

Chávez government has concerned the legacy of this civil–military relationship. Taxed with the criticism that his government owes its origin to a failed military coup, albeit one that took place some years before he was elected president, Chávez likes to recall that the progressive government of General Medina Angarita, for which he has some affection, was overthrown by a coup organized by Betancourt and the Acción Democrática party, a political grouping for which he has always had undisguised contempt. Betancourt, of course, is fondly remembered by his supporters as 'the father of Venezuelan democracy', yet his route to power was via a military coup.

Luís Miquilena is a living witness to the arguments of that era. 'There was a certain process of political development in Venezuela,' he recalls, 'which began with the replacement of the dictatorship of Juan Vicente Gómez by General López Contreras; this later moved forward considerably with Medina Angarita, who opened the doors to democracy.'

General Medina ruled Venezuela during the boom years of the Second World War, when the allied powers were keen to secure their supplies of Venezuelan oil. He obtained important concessions from the foreign oil companies, and was supported by the Communist Party. A positive memory of his government is still firmly upheld by sections of the left. Yet his otherwise rather progressive policies were not supported by the oil workers, whose union rights were restricted in order to ensure that strikes did not interfere with wartime production. Acción Democrática, supporting the rights of the workers, soon became the dominant political force in the oil fields. Fearing that the Communists might make common cause with Medina Angarita's chosen successor, Betancourt and Acción Democrática decided on a coup in October 1944.

Miquilena, who describes himself as 'a fighter for social rights who took an active part in the trade union struggle', had taken a benign attitude towards Medina Angarita, though unlike the orthodox Communists at the time he did not wish to actively support his government. When it was under threat, however, he was actively hostile to the military uprising against it. 'I played my part, in support of

Medina, against the uprising of Acción Democrática, to try to prevent this military action from succeeding.'

Medina Angarita was overthrown, yet, as Miquilena points out, the coup proved a mixed blessing for its organizers. Betancourt and Acción Democrática (and their president, Rómulo Gallegos) enjoyed the fruits of their coup for a brief spell of three years, from 1945 to 1948, but their government was then itself overthrown in 1948 by Pérez Jiménez, who ruled for a decade. 'Acción Democrática was forced to endure its disastrous consequences during a dictatorship that lasted for ten years, and ensured the absence of all civil liberties.'

To understand the history of today, these detours into the obscurities of the past are almost inevitable. The trajectory of Luís Miquilena, a politician with a long history of dissent, is particularly illuminating, for he is the man who has helped to revive the tradition of socialist nationalism that lies at the heart of the project of Hugo Chávez. In 1944, when still a union leader, Miquilena formed part of an anti-Stalinist Communist group known as the 'Machamíques', at a time when the orthodox Communist Party had joined forces with Medina Angarita. It had done so towards the end of the war, under instructions from the United States Communists led by Earl Browder (and, by extension, from America's ally in Moscow, Joseph Stalin). Moscow wanted no actions that would upset its Western ally.

Miquilena and the Machado brothers, Gustavo and Eduardo, both Communists, were opposed to this position (hence the name 'Machamíques'). They thought that policy should be made in Venezuela, not in Moscow – and still less in the United States. Miquilena helped to set up a new anti-Stalinist Communist Party in 1946, called the Partido Comunista Venezolano Unitario. His party was known at the time as 'los negros' (the blacks), because in the distribution of election colours (essential in a largely illiterate population) the orthodox Communist Party had secured the colour red.

The chief organizer of 'los negros', and the pioneering creator of socialist nationalism in Venezuela, was Salvador de la Plaza, a little-known history lecturer at the Universidad Central in Caracas who died in 1970 at the age of 74. Yet this forgotten figure, known to his students as 'the red monk', is one of the intellectual authors of the project of Hugo Chávez. Indeed it is impossible to understand the historical roots of Chávez's success without reference to the powerful anti-Stalinist communism of de la Plaza and Miquilena that was to influence important sections of the Venezuelan left in the years since the 1940s. Miquilena remains the most significant spokesman of this tradition, though it touched some of the other participants in the Patriotic Front of 1989.

Apart from Miquilena, the core of its membership consisted of Douglas Bravo, the guerrilla leader from the 1960s; Manuel Quijada, a lawyer involved in the military rebellions of 1962; Lino Martínez, another former guerrilla fighter, later to be a minister in Chávez's government; and Lieutenant William Izarra, the Marxist revolutionary who had recently retired from the air force.

The Front had issued a series of pamphlets, called 'Three decades of frustration', which made a certain impact in the newspapers. Among its more concrete proposals was that a Constituent Assembly should be held to prepare a new constitution, a recommendation that was eventually to become an essential plank in the political programme of Chávez. Yet the membership of the Front was too diverse and too politically divided to last out the year, and Chávez later described it as 'stillborn': 'A Patriotic Front cannot be invented; you cannot assemble a hundred distinguished figures and say "We are the Front". I don't believe in that.'

Yet the composition of the Front of 1989 was an important pointer to the years ahead, for several of its members were to become key supporters of the Chávez government in 1999. One of the civilian leftists involved was Pedro Duno, a philosophy professor at the Universidad Central in Caracas, and always an influential figure on the left. Duno, who came from a military family, kept up his contacts within the military over the years. He died in November 1998 just after being elected senator for Miranda state as a supporter of Chávez. Writing in *Ultimas Noticias* on 23 June 1991, two years after the *Caracazo*, he had prepared the intellectual ground for a new coup:

Venezuela is a country in an advanced state of collapse, whose characteristics of corruption and pillage, incompetence, irresponsibility and cynicism, define the gloomy panorama of the present. In this bleak situation it is being suggested that the armed forces should intervene. Since it is impossible to use the force of reasonable argument, or of law, or of rights, or of the constitution, because the state and the government provide no guarantees, then it will be justifiable to use the reasonable argument of force, the *ultima ratio*.

Just over six months later, on 4 February 1992, Colonel Chávez took him at his word.

9

TORRÍJOS, VELASCO AND THE TRADITION
OF MILITARY REBELLION IN
LATIN AMERICA

A generation of young officers . . . decided not just to organize a coup d'etat, but to do away with the entire system of apparent 'democracy' in the country. People had grown accustomed to mixing up politics with their economic activity, using their democratic freedom in much the same way as women use cosmetics.

General Omar Torríjos, August 1975

More than a quarter of a century ago, in 1974, I went to visit General Omar Torríjos, the military ruler of Panama. I flew to his seaside dacha by the shores of the Pacific and we spent all day talking. There were just four of us: the head of the secret service, the rector of the university, Torríjos and I. The general lay in his hammock for most of the day, in a shaded patio overlooking the sea, sometimes talkative and sometimes taciturn. Much of the time we talked about peasants and land reform, and about what had happened in the rural areas of China and Chile, of Vietnam and Peru, and Cuba. Torríjos was a great admirer of Fidel, but he said that he didn't agree with everything being done there. 'They should have left the peasants with a little piece of land they could call their own.'

As Graham Greene was to find, it was difficult not to be captivated by this enchanting figure, the complete antithesis of the Latin American officer in dark glasses. Torríjos had seized power in 1968, and was to rule Panama for thirteen years until he was killed in an air crash in 1981. He had a radical programme of reform, chiefly related to the Canal Zone, the chunk of Panamanian territory that the Americans had expropriated in 1903. The zone had subsequently been directly controlled by the US Department of Defense, later the Pentagon, and used for the construction of an inter-oceanic canal and innumerable military bases. But Torríjos' political programme went beyond the nationalist issue of the Canal. He rebelled against the corruption of the political elite, and he pushed through a land reform to try to benefit the peasants.

The history of Latin America in the 1970s and 1980s was so dominated by the eruption of military dictatorships of the right that it is easy to forget the existence of another tradition. For on many occasions, in the nineteenth as well as the twentieth century, radical officers have appeared with the interests of the people at heart, ready to do battle on their behalf with local landlords or foreign capitalists. Manuel Isidoro Belzú in Bolivia, Ezequiel Zamora in Venezuela, Luis Carlos Prestes in Brazil, Marmaduke Grove in Chile – there is a long and infinitely fascinating list.

When members of the old Venezuelan political elite come together to discuss the Chávez phenomenon, they like to examine the example of countries where military rule was imposed on civilian societies by left-wing nationalist officers – both in Latin America and elsewhere. The favoured foreign examples are Kemal Ataturk in Turkey and Gamel Abdul Nasser in Egypt, with occasional references to Charles de Gaulle in France. Closer to home, the 'usual suspects' under consideration are Omar Torríjos in Panama, Juan Velasco Alvarado in Peru, and Juan Domingo Perón in Argentina. The government of Colonel Chávez, it is always assumed, is going to take one of these roads.

Although democracy rather than military rule became the dominant practice in Latin America in the 1990s, this was not always so. There have been few periods in the continent's history in which military officers have not played a pivotal role, though most of them have come from the right rather than the left.

The ruling elites of the continent have always held ambivalent views about their armed forces. On the one hand, the military are remembered as the essential and historic bulwark against the rebellious indigenous Indian population whose lands were stolen by settlers over the centuries. In this context, the soldiers appear as the saviours of the nation to whom the descendants of the settlers are expected to register their eternal gratitude. Since the descendants of the indigenous peoples now populate the inflated and explosive urban shanty towns of the continent, and continue to pose a similar, though different, threat to the heirs to the settler class, gratitude to the armed forces remains high on the agenda.

On the other hand, while the military may be useful or even essential to the ruling elites, they are also perceived to represent an inferior social class that is always held in low esteem. Officers are often the butt of endless jokes. The excesses of the military dictatorships of the 1970s and 1980s gave the military everywhere a bad name, and today's elites, whether of ancient lineage or newly emerging from the universities, now tend to regard the armed forces as a necessary evil, best kept corralled in their barracks. This view has been reinforced by the government of the United States in the 1990s, in complete contradiction to earlier American policies which favoured strong military dictatorships over effete civilian regimes.

The Americans used to fear that democratic governments would be dominated by nationalists, leftists or social democrats, people insufficiently mindful of American economic or strategic interests. This was often the case. Throughout the 1970s and into the 1980s, the United States was content to see much of Latin America fall under conservative military rule, and encouraged the process. A pattern begun in Brazil in 1964 was continued in Chile in September 1973, when General Augusto Pinochet overthrew the elected government of Salvador Allende. The tradition was sustained in Bolivia and Uruguay in the 1970s, and reached a low point in March 1976 with the coup in Argentina by General Jorge Videla, who overthrew the government of María Estela, the widow of General Perón.

These regimes were noted for their flagrant disregard for human rights, but the generals enjoyed the warm support of the government in Washington. Their firm stand in support of the traditional economic interests of the United States, and their rigidly anti-Communist position in the Cold War, overrode any doubts about their domestic repression. The kind of tough, centralized government provided by the military, which forebade workers from uniting in trade unions, was much appreciated by foreign capital.

In the 1990s, however, with the development of a new kind of neo-liberal economics that had no need of tough military government, and with an end to the strategic emergency imposed by the Cold War, Washington began to favour democracy. The trademark dark glasses of the military dictators were no longer in fashion.

Yet there was an alternative tradition, and Colonel Chávez had always taken an interest in the experience of General Torríjos and General Velasco of Peru. He had met the son of Torríjos who had taken part in a military training course in Venezuela, and he had read some of the political material relating to the transformations in Panama that Torríjos junior had brought with him. Some of yesterday's rhetoric by Torríjos is echoed by Chávez today.

Interviewed in August 1975, Torríjos had sought to justify his coup d'etat on the grounds that the Panamanian National Guard, which he led, had been transformed into 'the wage-slaves of the oligarchy':

> Our mission was to maintain the status quo, with blood and thunder, with timely military deployment, or with a coup d'etat. I was forced to take part in acts of repression, indeed I got sick of so much repression. As a direct result, the National Guard decided to rebel, to decolonize the country. Above all, we wanted to solve the problem of the canal, which for the Panamanians was almost a religion.

As was to happen in Venezuela, the Panamanian officers had rebelled against what they perceived as the incompetence and corruption of the civilian rulers:

We were the sentries of the oligarchy until the mistakes of the politicians became so serious that there was no prospect of rectification. A generation of young officers, graduates of the Panamanian Military School, decided not just to organize a coup d'etat, but to do away with the entire system of apparent 'democracy' in the country. People had grown accustomed to mixing up politics with their economic activity, using their democratic freedom in much the same way as women use cosmetics.

Torríjos succeeded in wrenching a new canal treaty from the United States government of Jimmy Carter in 1979, and the Panama Canal was eventually handed over to the Panamanians 20 years later, in December 1999. But Torríjos did not live to see this cardinal event; he was killed in an air crash in August 1981. His successor, Manuel Noriega, handled matters with less diplomatic aplomb, and suffered the indignity of an American invasion in 1989 – 'Operation Just Cause' – in which more than 1,000 Panamanians were killed. He was captured, accused of drug smuggling and money laundering, and is still serving a lifetime's sentence in an American prison.

Equally influential in the political formation of Colonel Chávez has been the nationalist experiment of the Peruvian military during the government of General Velasco between 1968 and 1976. He had visited Peru as a young cadet in 1974, although at a time when Velasco's 'Revolutionary Government of the Armed Forces' was already in sharp decline. He claims to have been influenced by the Peruvian example, though the Peruvian experience actually bears little comparison with the project on which he has embarked in Venezuela – though a few of its lessons might still be learnt.

As in Venezuela and Panama, a group of intelligent Peruvian officers, unhappy about corruption and the state of the country, had been discussing the possibility of a military intervention. Some of them had been influenced by their experience in France during the Algerian war. As in Venezuela, these officers held their country's principal political party – Apra in Peru, Acción Democrática in Venezuela – in great distrust, partly because of its overtly anti-nationalist and pro-American position. As in Venezuela, the Peruvian officers had had experience of an anti-guerrilla war and were more aware than civilian politicians of the abject conditions of the population in the rural areas.

When they seized power in 1968, the Peruvian military announced their intention of building a new order that would be 'neither capitalist nor communist'. Their particular concern at that moment was the corruption of the civilian regime of Fernándo Belaúnde Terry, the devaluation of the currency, and a clause in a government contract signed with an American oil company, Standard Oil, that appeared contrary to the national interest. Inflation, low by Latin American standards, but unusually high for Peru, was running at 19 per cent.

The reformist zeal of General Velasco derived in part from his experience in crushing the Peruvian guerrilla movements of the 1960s. His first-hand knowledge of the sufferings of the rural population of the Andes, which the guerrillas of Hugo Blanco and Luís de la Puente Uceda had sought to redress, led him to adopt much of the guerrilla programme as his own. Velasco was an officer of high intelligence, influenced by the example of General de Gaulle in France, where he had served as a military attaché in the years immediately after the end of the Algerian war.

Velasco nationalized the foreign oil companies, expropriated the sugar haciendas, and carried out an extensive land reform, and made Quechua, the language of the Andes, an official language of the country. He also expropriated the conservative newspapers, and encouraged worker participation in the management of state industries. To the annoyance of Washington, he re-established diplomatic relations with Cuba, and engaged in a growing bilateral trade with the Soviet Union.

In retrospect, as Richard Webb, the governor of the Peruvian central bank in the successor regime, has recalled, Velasco's economic programme was not quite as radical as it once had seemed:

> The military regime carried out deep social, institutional, and economic reforms, many of them applauded by the Washington

consensus of the time. Indeed much of the reform agenda, in particular the land reform, the educational reform, and the reinforcement of the planning mechanisms, seemed to come straight from the books of the earlier Alliance for Progress and from standard World Bank prescriptions of the time.

The Velasco government suffered from two fundamental flaws: after a period of initial enthusiasm, it lacked popular support; and it tried to carry out a revolution on borrowed money. These two flaws, implicit from the start, proved the cause of its downfall. The government had no civilian presence; it was entirely composed of officers; and it never reached out to sectors beyond the immediate beneficiaries of Velasco's reforms.

The lack of money was even more serious. In 1976, Peru had exhausted its foreign reserves, and had to seek a foreign loan from a consortium of American banks. The conditions imposed were impressive: a wage freeze, devaluation and budget cuts in the public sector; the abolition of the right to strike; the sacking from the government of its more prominent radical members; an end to the ban on oil contracts with foreign firms; and the sale of state companies to the private sector.

Not surprisingly, the Velasco regime ran into deep trouble. After his death in 1977, there was severe rioting and a prolonged police strike. Perceiving the depths of public hostility, his conservative successor, General Francisco Morales Bermúdez, was persuaded to abandon the entire project and to return the country to civilian rule. After fresh elections in 1980, Belaúnde Terry, the politician so rudely deposed in 1968, was re-elected president, and soon the memory of the military revolution was rubbed out.

The military governments of Peru and Panama have often been derided by journalists and political scientists. Both Velasco and Torríjos set off with high hopes of redeeming the conditions of the poor and 'standing up' to the local big power in the Americas. Both were serious and intelligent leaders possessed of considerable charisma. Their deaths were mourned as a national catastrophe. They could not be faulted for their ambition, yet they were unable to sustain the revolutionary programmes they had put in train.

Colonel Chávez follows in their footsteps, but with a different agenda and having learnt from their mistakes. He is an elected president, not a military dictator. He knows that a revolution cannot succeed on borrowed money, and he knows that the armed forces cannot rule on their own. They need the support of the great mass of the people.

PART TWO

RECOVERING THE PAST

10

THE LEGACY OF SIMÓN BOLÍVAR

You are the man of destiny. Nothing that has happened in the past
bears any resemblance to your accomplishments. To imitate you,
it would be necessary once again to liberate a world. You have
created five republics, an achievement which . . . shall lift your
image to a height never yet reached by any human being. Your
glory will grow with the centuries, as the shadows grow when the
sun is setting.

José Domingo Choquehuanca to Bolívar, 1825

Wherever you go in Venezuela, and in much of Latin America as well,
an image can always be found of Simón Bolívar, liberator of the
country (and a large part of the continent) from Spanish rule. It may
be a statue in a town square, a painting in a minister's office, or a scrib-
ble on the wall. You can never entirely escape from the noble brow,
the slightly supercilious curve of the smile, and, if the artist is honest,
the sallow complexion of the skin that indicates a *zambo*, a man of
mixed race.

Traditional Venezuelan histories have always emphasized
Bolívar's aristocratic origins rather than his black heritage. Yet Bolívar
stood up for the rights of Venezuela's large community of black slaves.

During the fight for independence, he had sought assistance in 1816 from President Alexandre Pétion, black ruler of the free slave republic of Haiti. Pétion agreed to provide it if Bolívar would promise to liberate the slaves of Venezuela. Bolívar had already freed the slaves on his own estates, but he could make no impact on the reactionary slave-owning class of post-independence Venezuela, and slave freedom did not finally come until 1854.

The secular cult of Bolívar has survived unchanged in Venezuela over many generations. Successive presidents and generals, the corrupt, the idle and the patriotic, have all bowed down in obedient homage to the Liberator. At the end of the twentieth century, Hugo Chávez has proved to be no exception. He has erected the example and the thoughts of Bolívar almost to the level of an ideology, renaming the country in the new constitution of 1999 as the 'Bolívarian Republic of Venezuela'.

Yet this is not, as Chávez is often at pains to emphasize, an exercise in mindless nationalism. His purpose is not just to venerate a figure to whom most of his predecessors have only paid lip-service, but also to rescue the historical character and achievements of the Liberator from the accretions of myth and fable.

He has not been alone in this. A similar task has been undertaken by several writers in recent years. One internationally famous effort was the novel about Bolívar's final months, *The General in his Labyrinth*, written by Gabriel García Márquez, the Colombian writer who won the Nobel Prize for Literature, and first published in 1989. This was a fictional account of the last year of the Liberator's life, in 1830, when he was already out of power and his life's work appeared to have crumbled around him. The novel created a human dimension to the conventional bronze statue.

Another influential book within intellectual circles in Venezuela and Colombia was *El culto a Bolívar* by the Venezuelan historian Germán Carrera Damas. This also made a stab at demystifying Bolívar's career, but was not well received, Chávez recalls, by the senior officers at the military academy in Caracas. Chávez himself warmed to this rewriting of received history and used the debate about

Bolívar's role in the past in his own classes at the academy, seeking to recover some of the characteristics of the Liberator that might be of political value in the present. His aim was to draw on the country's historical traditions to help lay out a pattern for the future.

The example of Bolívar's career has been of particular service to Chávez in his examination of a possible role for Venezuela in the affairs of the rest of the continent. Most Latin American politicians have long recognized that their nation states are too weak to operate on their own. This has been the common view in the continent for several decades, and had provided the basic political push behind the drive towards economic integration. Bolívar had faced a similar problem, and drew the conclusion that it would be necessary to promote a continent-wide crusade against Spanish imperial rule, uniting Latin America against the outside power.

Chávez now seeks to do something similar. His aim is to re-ignite the Bolívarian dream, to seek the political unification of Latin America on a new basis: the internal integration of each country. To this end, he plans a great conference of the 'Bolívarian' states, those liberated by Bolívar, to replicate the one that Bolívar organized in Panama in 1826. 'A valid project for the twenty-first century,' Chávez believes passionately, 'is to bring together at a conference the balkanized countries of Latin America.'

Bolívar is not the only significant figure that Chávez has resurrected from the past. In the 1980s, in discussion with junior officers, his closest military friends, he began to rescue the thoughts and writings of other protagonists in Venezuela's nineteenth-century history, notably Simón Rodríguez and Ezequiel Zamora. He has included them in the pantheon of his embryonic revolutionary movement. In the process, he found himself to be participating in the historical debate about the nineteenth century that had been going on within the Venezuelan left since the 1960s.

The original view of the Marxist left, in Venezuela as elsewhere, was one of extreme hostility to Bolívar. Taking their cue from the writings of Marx himself, most Marxist writers perceived the Liberator as a typically bourgeois figure whose actions had only served the interests of the emergent imperial power of the time. Bolívar, according to this reading, had secured independence from Spain with English support. He had then handed over the continent to exploitation by English capitalism. For years, this caricature portrait of Bolívar as an imperialist stooge effectively precluded the left from examining any of his more positive characteristics. It was impossible for anyone on the left to perceive him as a revolutionary model for the twentieth century.

In the course of the 1960s, in Venezuela, this view had already begun to change. The guerrilla movements had given their military units the names of heroes from the past: José Leonardo Chirinos, the leader of an eighteenth-century slave revolt in Coro; and Ezequiel Zamora, the leader of the peasantry in the *llanos* in the nineteenth century. Later, when some of the guerrillas split away from the orthodox Communist party, they began to re-examine what they had learnt about the past with a view to creating an ideology of the left with a heavier dose of nationalism – just as Chávez was to do in subsequent years.

Among their number was Douglas Bravo, commander of the 'José Leonardo Chirinos' guerrilla group in Falcón state. Bravo claims today that his expulsion from the Communist Party, in June 1965, was partly due to his arguments in favour of the ideas of the heroes of the nineteenth century – Bolívar, Simón Rodríguez, and Ezequiel Zamora among them. Their notions ran directly contrary to Soviet orthodoxy.

Bravo formed a new political party in April 1966, the Partido de la Revolución Venezolano (PRV), infused with the ideas of these figures from the past. He recalls that the party's chief philosopher, Pedro Duno, had published a document in 1969 entitled 'Marxism-Leninism-Bolívarianism'. Duno's aim was to 'nationalize' the ideology of the Latin American left. As well as reviving the figure of the Liberator, Bravo's party was also attracted to the key idea of Simón Rodríguez that '[Latin] America should not slavishly imitate, but should seek to be original.'

When Chávez started to organize his military conspiracy in the 1980s and made his first contacts with the revolutionary left, he found that they were already talking the same language. The resurrection of Bolívar as an important and necessary forerunner of any future radical revolution was accepted by the leftists that he met.

Although Bolívar is widely recognized as one of the great figures of the nineteenth century, few people outside Latin America retain anything more than a few anecdotal details about his life and work. He is probably most famous for the sad reflection that he made at the end of his life that he had 'ploughed the sea'. Yet since the figure of Bolívar is a significant item in the political project of Hugo Chávez, and recurs so frequently in his rhetoric, it is necessary to include here a brief account of his life and achievements.

Born on 24 July 1783 in Caracas, Bolívar died in Colombia before he was fifty, on 17 December 1830. The principal leader of the Latin American rebellions against the Spanish empire, he fought for the liberation of Venezuela and Colombia, as well as Ecuador, Peru, and Upper Peru (Bolivia), and his campaigns spanned a period of more than ten years. He fought backwards and forwards across Venezuela, up and down Colombia, and then made an inspired march down the Andes into Ecuador and Peru. Not since the battles of the first generation of conquistadors in the sixteenth century had a single general covered so much ground with such far-reaching results.

Bolívar was also something of an intellectual. Widely read in the classics and the recent emancipatory literature of pre-revolutionary France, he maintained a voluminous correspondence that reveals a man of sharp wit and observation. Many of his 'open letters' and speeches remain as models of the advanced political thought of the time.

At the same time, he was a man of harsh and uncompromising views, often cruel and unpredictable in his actions. He made many mistakes, both tactical and strategic, and his entire project was frequently on the verge of collapse. He believed very firmly that he was in charge of an anarchic continent that would benefit from strong leadership. Arrogant and almost certainly insufferable, he had no doubt that he himself was that necessary leader.

Bolívar's parents died when he was quite young, and he lived for a while in the house of his tutor, Simón Rodríguez, another significant figure in the Chávez pantheon who will reappear in the next chapter. Bolívar travelled as a young adult to Europe, first to Spain between 1798 and 1801, and then to France and Italy between 1804 and 1807. Stimulated by the revolutionary atmosphere of the time, he devoured the works of Voltaire and Rousseau, and when he returned to Venezuela in 1807, he devoted himself to its embryonic and clandestine independence movement.

An uprising occurred in Caracas on 19 April 1810 which forced the resignation of the Spanish captain-general. A revolutionary junta assumed power in the city and sent Bolívar to England to secure British support for their regime. Arriving in London in July, at the height of the Napoleonic wars, Bolívar failed to interest the British government in the fate of his country, but he had some success in persuading the exiled Francisco de Miranda to return with him to Caracas, to take command of the revolutionary forces. Miranda, who had fought in the ranks of the French Revolution, had made an earlier attempt to organize a rebellion against Spain in 1806.

On his return to Caracas, Bolívar joined the republican army and was given command of the strategically important port city of Puerto Cabello. Venezuela's independence was formally declared on 5 July 1811, after a congress had gathered in Caracas in March to draft a constitution for the new republic.

Ten years of fighting now lay ahead, for the Spanish did not accept this republican rebellion in Caracas and still controlled other parts of the country – and the continent. Their counter-attack was not long in coming, presaged in March 1812 by a serious earthquake which destroyed much of the city. The Catholic Church, ever hostile to the republican regime and loyal to Madrid, soon made political capital out of the disaster, just as prominent clergymen were to do after the terrible mudslide disaster in Caracas and Vargas state in December 1999.

The republican forces were weak and ill-armed, and divided among themselves. Soon they were on the defensive: the Spaniards recaptured Puerto Cabello when Bolívar was looking the other way; and Miranda attempted to make peace with the Spanish commander in Caracas. Denouncing Miranda as a traitor, the republicans handed him over to the Spaniards. He was taken in chains to Spain, and died in prison in Cadiz.

Bolívar, meanwhile, had escaped by sea from Venezuela and arrived at the port of Cartagena in New Granada (now Colombia), then an enclave under the control of independent republicans. There he published the first of his great political statements, the Cartagena Manifesto, calling for the destruction of Spanish power in Venezuela as a prelude to continental unification, and demanding that it be replaced by strong centralized government:

> Government must prove to be formidable and ruthless, without regard to law or constitution, until peace is established. I believe that our enemies will have all the advantages as long as we do not unify our American government. We shall be inextricably caught in the web of civil war, and be shamefully beaten by that little horde of bandits which pollutes our country.

Taking him at his word, the republicans in Cartagena chose Bolívar to be the commander of an expeditionary force that would secure the liberation of Venezuela. Embarking on a three-month campaign, he defeated the Spanish army in several battles, and recaptured Caracas on 6 August 1813. The reconvened Congress gave him the title of 'Liberator'.

It was a fleeting victory, the republican forces did not hold Caracas for long. With the end of the Napoleonic wars in Europe, the Spaniards sent fresh troops out to Latin America, and in General José Tomás Boves, they had a skilled and ruthless commander, able to mobilize the Indians and peasants of the *llanos* into a fighting force capable of matching those of Bolívar. Boves captured Caracas a year later, in July 1814, exacted exemplary punishment, and closed a chapter in the history of the independent Venezuelan republic.

Bolívar escaped again to Cartagena, and in December he captured Bogotá. But the arrival of a fresh Spanish army from Europe brought new defeats, and in May 1815, he was obliged to move on to Jamaica.

Here he wrote, in his 'Letter from Jamaica', a visionary plan for the future of Latin America, embracing the entire continent, from Argentina and Chile to Mexico:

> We are a macrocosm of the human race. We are a world apart, confined within two oceans, young in art and science, but old as human society. We are neither Indians nor Europeans, yet we are a part of each other.

Bolívar tried to return to Cartagena, but discovering that it had fallen again into Spanish hands, his ship turned towards the independent black republic of Haiti. Arriving at Port au Prince on 1 January 1816, he was welcomed by President Pétion, who agreed to provide him with arms and ammunition, and allowed him to recruit sailors for his invasion fleet.

Launching an attack on Venezuela from Haiti was always going to be a risky operation, and it proved a disaster. Bolívar's fleet captured the island of Margarita, but was repelled from the mainland in July 1816 at Carupano and at Ocumare. He retreated to Haiti, to prepare a second expedition, and towards the end of the year, he returned to the Venezuelan mainland, at Barcelona.

The war against the Spaniards now entered a new phase. In April 1817, Bolívar sailed round the coast to the delta of the Orinoco. Advancing up river, he established his headquarters in July at Angostura (now Ciudad Bolívar). Here he made contact with republican leaders in the *llanos*, notably with José Antonio Páez and Francisco de Paula Santander from the Colombian border. Bolívar's forces now fought in the *llanos* over a long two-year period, until finally they were ready to launch an attack on Colombia.

In 1819, Bolívar's forces climbed the mountain passes from the *llanos* into what was still the Spanish vice-royalty of New Granada. The royalist officers could not believe that the republican assault would come from this direction. Unprepared, they were defeated at the battle of Boyacá on 7 August. Three days later, Bolívar entered

Bogotá, while the Spanish viceroy escaped to the sea at Cartagena. Colombia was in the hands of the republicans.

Leaving General Santander in charge in Bogotá, as the vice-president for New Granada, Bolívar retraced his steps, climbing back down the slopes of the Andes, and sailing down the Apure to the Orinoco. In December he arrived at his old base at Angostura, and summoned the Congress to tell it of his triumphs:

> The union of New Granada and Venezuela is the goal that I set for myself even in my earliest fighting days. It is the desire of all the citizens of both countries, and would give the assurance of South American freedom.

Soon Ecuador was to be thrown in for good measure. The Angostura Congress appointed Bolívar to be the president and military dictator of the new state, to be called the Republic of Gran Colombia. It was designed to be a federation of the old Spanish 'departments' of Venezuela and New Granada (Colombia), and Quito (Ecuador).

For several months there was a truce, but in June 1821, Bolívar's men advanced north from the Orinoco and defeated the Spanish army at the battle of Carabobo. The way was open to Caracas, and Bolívar arrived at night in triumph. The liberation of Venezuela was now complete. A new congress assembled on the border, at Cúcuta, to draft a constitution for the new republic and to formally elect Bolívar as president in September 1821.

Bolívar was now the ruler of the joint republic of Venezuela and Colombia, with a duty to be the Liberator of Latin America. He did not linger long in Caracas. He had wider ambitions. He had sent one of his officers, General Antonio José de Sucre, south that year to assist in the liberation of Ecuador. Sucre had gone to the Pacific port at Guayaquil, and was now in need of assistance.

Again leaving Santander in charge in Bogotá, Bolívar marched south in December 1821, along the mountain road towards Quito, the capital of Ecuador. His military campaign against the forces of Spain had still not finished. While Bolívar advanced from the north, Sucre advanced inland from the west, from the coast at Guayaquil. Sucre's forces defeated the Spanish army at the battle of Pichincha on 24 May 1822, and Quito fell the following day. Bolívar arrived three weeks later, on 16 June, and then moved down to Guayaquil.

The three territories of Gran Colombia had now been liberated from Spanish rule. Argentina and Chile were also free, conquered by revolutionary forces from Argentina led by General José de San Martín. Only Peru now remained under Spanish control.

San Martín had marched into Lima from the south, and proclaimed Peruvian independence, but Spanish soldiers still controlled the cities of the Andes. San Martín now travelled to Guayaquil to seek Bolívar's help in what would be the final attack on the Spanish army. The two generals met there on 26 July 1822. San Martín clearly needed assistance not just to defeat the Spanish but also to regain control over his own divided Argentine forces stationed in Lima. Bolívar was clearly reluctant to take his side, and San Martín returned to Lima without receiving the help he had hoped for. He resigned all his positions, and left for exile in Europe, never to return.

A year later, in September 1823, Bolívar returned to Lima to prepare the final defeat of the Spanish army in the Andes. Assembling a fresh expeditionary force, he defeated the Spaniards at the battle of Junín in 1824. The campaign finally came to an end on 9 December, when the Spanish viceroy surrendered to General Sucre at the battle of Ayacucho.

Sucre pursued the remnants of the Spanish army south along the Andes and into the country of Upper Peru, which, finally liberated in April 1825, was given the name of Bolivia, in honour of the Liberator. Spanish Latin America was finally free.

Bolívar moved on towards the Potosí mountain in Bolivia, pausing to be addressed by José Domingo Choquehuanca, mayor of a small village on the frontier:

> You are the man of destiny. Nothing that has happened in the past bears any resemblance to your accomplishments. To imitate you,

it would be necessary once again to liberate a world. You have created five republics, an achievement which, in its unprecedented demand for their development, shall lift your image to a height never yet reached by any human being. Your glory will grow with the centuries, as the shadows grow when the sun is setting.

Gerhard Masur, Bolívar's biographer, thinks that this speech must be apocryphal, but since it is a legend that is now incrusted in Venezuela's history, as well as being one of Hugo Chavéz's favourite quotes, it deserves a place in this story.

Bolívar spent the remaining months of 1825 in Bolivia, returning at the end of the year to Lima, to be elected president of Peru in August 1826. His far-flung empire was now too large to be controlled by one general, as insoluble political problems arose in each separate state. Bolívar's dream of teaching Europe a lesson remained undimmed: 'Let us show Europe that America has men capable of emulating the glory of the heroes of the ancient world,' he told General Sucre, as he ordered him to take charge of Bolivia. Yet there was dissension in Peru, soon to be followed by war between Venezuela and Colombia. His two generals, Paez and Santander quarrelled, and the ambitious project of a united Gran Colombia evaporated in 1828. The union of the two countries was split asunder, and in 1829, the Peruvians invaded Ecuador in an attempt to capture Guayaquil.

Bolívar made one final effort to secure the political union of Latin America, at a congress of Spanish-speaking states held in Panama in 1826. There were many absentees, and only Peru, Gran Colombia and representatives from Mexico and Central America took part. Political union was on the agenda and the states present agreed to plan for a joint army and navy, but all such concrete schemes were stillborn. All that remained of the Congress of Panama was a vision of what might one day be. Bolívar died of tuberculosis in December 1830, near Santa Marta in Colombia, on his way into exile in Europe. 'America is ungovernable,' he said at the end. 'Those in the service of the revolution have ploughed the sea.'

Hugo Chávez does not share Bolívar's pessimism. 'The contradictions in Bolívar's thought are not the determining factor,' he argues. 'What we can see in the period of history between 1810 and 1830 are the outlines of a national project for Spanish America.' That project was taken up again, on occasion, notably by Ezequiel Zamora, a quarter of a century after Bolívar's death. Chávez now plans to put it back onto the continental agenda.

11

ROBINSON CRUSOE AND THE
PHILOSOPHY OF SIMÓN RODRÍGUEZ

Oh, my teacher, my friend, my Robinson, you are in Colombia,
you are in Bogotá, and you have not told me!

Bolívar to Simón Rodríguez, 1824

Hugo Chávez often refers to the 'Robinsonian system', and I thought
at first that perhaps he was thinking of the work of the late Joan
Robinson, the distinguished Cambridge economist with whom
Latin American intellectuals were certainly familiar in the 1960s
and 1970s. Then, inevitably, I thought of Robinson Crusoe, the
fictional hero of Daniel Defoe, who hailed originally from York and
lived for 'Eight and Twenty Years all alone in an uninhabited Island
on the Coast of America, near the Mouth of the Great River of
OROONOQUE.'

That turned out to be nearer the mark. The political and economic
thinking of Hugo Chávez does indeed derive in part, by a circuitous
route, from the story of Robinson Crusoe and the impact that it made
on Simón Rodríguez, a young Caracas school-teacher in the 1790s.
Rodríguez was first the teacher and later the close friend of Simón
Bolívar, and the radical philosophy both men espoused, one influenc-
ing the other, lies at the heart of the Chávez project for Venezuela and

for Latin America. Rodríguez was so struck by the character of Robinson Crusoe that he changed his name to Samuel Robinson.

The life and works of Simón Rodríguez are almost unknown outside Latin America, and his writings have never been translated into English, yet he had influence in several countries, living and working in Venezuela and Colombia, in Chile and Bolivia, and in Peru and Ecuador. He was a school-teacher and an educational philosopher, and a man with unorthodox ideas about education and commerce. He also had a passionate belief in the need to integrate the indigenous peoples of Latin America, and the black slaves brought from outside, into the societies of the future independent states. Two hundred years later, his words and ideas have a contemporary ring – and have been resurrected by Hugo Chávez.

Daniel Defoe's story about Robinson Crusoe's adventures was based on the true life adventures of Alexander Selkirk, who was marooned on the Juan Fernández island in the Pacific. Defoe simply changed the island to one in the Atlantic, off the Orinoco river. The book was first published in London in 1719, and translated into French and Dutch the following year. It must eventually have been available on the banks of the Orinoco itself, in Venezuela, although it is possible that Latin Americans first read the German version of the story written by Joachim Heinrich Campe. *Robinson der Jüngere* by Campe was first published in Hamburg in 1769, and was destined to become one of the most famous German books of all time. It was written under the influence of Rousseau's *Emile or Education*, which had indicated that Robinson Crusoe was a most excellent book for children in that it taught them to learn as Robinson had done, by doing.

Whichever version of the story arrived in Caracas, it was read by Simón Rodríguez, the teacher in charge of the town council's primary school. Among his young pupils, and at one stage his lodger, was Simón Bolívar, the orphaned son of a wealthy land-owning family.

Rodríguez was born in Caracas in October 1769, and his first primary school soon ran into trouble with the city fathers. He had written and published a long memorandum suggesting that his school should not only be for the children of wealthy whites, but for the children of blacks and *pardos* too. This concern with the underclass remained with him all his life, and caused him endless pain and trouble. He was a hundred years ahead of his time. Years later, when working in Bolivia in the 1820s, he was to insist that the children of Indians should be provided with free education in the public schools he was setting up. The authorities soon found an excuse to close them down.

Dismissed by the Caracas council, Rodríguez became involved in the early independence movement of 1797, organized by Manuel Gual and José María España. When this premature revolt was crushed, Rodríguez was forced into exile. He sailed across the Caribbean to Jamaica, arriving a couple of years after the British colonial government had crushed a great Maroon rebellion. In Jamaica he learned English. He thought of his new home as 'the island of Robinson Crusoe', and, anxious to shake off his own Spanish antecedents, he changed his name to 'Samuel Robinson'. He kept the pseudonym for a quarter of a century, throughout the years he remained outside the continent.

Leaving Jamaica, he travelled on to the United States, and then to Europe. 'I stayed in Europe for more than twenty years,' he wrote years later when asked to describe his peregrinations. 'I worked in a laboratory as an industrial chemist where I learnt a thing or two; I joined a number of secret societies of a socialist nature . . . I studied a little literature, I learnt a few languages, and I taught in a primary school in a small village in Russia.'

Samuel Robinson might well have been an interesting but forgotten footnote in the intellectual history of Latin America had his path not crossed for a second time that of Simón Bolívar. The two men, teacher and pupil, met again in Napoleon's Paris in 1804, and they travelled on together to Italy. Through his friendship with Robinson, Bolívar met Alexander von Humboldt, the German scientist who had explored the Orinoco, and his tutor also gave him the writings of the Enlightenment to read. Years later, when fighting in Peru, Bolívar wrote of his feelings for his 'Robinson':

I love this man madly. He was my teacher and my travelling companion; he is a genius. He has an extraordinary wit, and a talent for learning and criticism . . . He is a teacher who instructs through entertaining, and a writer who instructs through example. He means everything to me. When I used to know him, he was worth the world. He would have to have changed a lot for me to be mistaken in my judgement.

While in Rome, in August 1805, these two independent-minded Venezuelans climbed the slopes of the 'Monte Sacro', the hilly promontory above the river Aniene north-east of Rome, where a bottling plant still dispenses *acqua santa* from an ancient spring. Here Bolívar took a romantic oath, swearing to devote his life to the independence struggle of Latin America. Long after Bolívar was dead, Rodríguez recalled the words of the oath and wrote them down, doubtless with some fictional embellishment. They remain deeply ingrained in the Venezuelan psyche, learnt by school-children and committed to memory by Venezuelan soldiers performing their military service. When Hugo Chávez came to organize a conspiracy of his own in the 1980s, it was to the words of Bolívar, remembered by Simón Rodríguez, that he turned:

I swear before you, and I swear before the God of my fathers, that I will not allow my arm to relax, nor my soul to rest, until I have broken the chains that oppress us . . .

Bolívar returned to South America a year later, in 1806, to take up the challenges of the independence struggle. Samuel Robinson remained behind, still intrigued by Napoleon's Europe. He set off on further travels, visiting and living in Italy and Germany, Prussia and Poland, and Russia. Somewhere along the way he must have joined the 'secret societies of a socialist nature' that he writes about.

Eventually, in 1823, he abandoned his Russian school, and arrived in London. There, in the house in Grafton Way that had once belonged to Francisco Miranda, he met another Latin American exile, Andrés

Bello, the Venezuelan philosopher. Bello, who was also an education-alist, encouraged him to return home, now that Latin America's inde-pendence was almost secured.

Samuel Robinson, by then aged 54, sailed back across the Atlantic, landed at the Colombian port of Cartagena, and changed his name back to Simón Rodríguez. Travelling on to Bogotá, he received news from Bolívar, who was then engaged in the conquest of Peru: 'Oh, my teacher, my friend, my Robinson, you are in Colombia, you are in Bogotá, and you have not told me!' Bolívar urged him to hurry down to meet him in Lima. The two old friends were reunited in Lima in 1824, shortly after the battle of Ayacucho which settled the fate of the Spanish empire in Latin America.

We do not know exactly what they discussed, though we do have a very clear picture of how the ideas of Simón Rodríguez developed in the years after his return to Latin America from Europe. His Euro-pean experience had convinced him that America would have to try to do things differently. In one of his first books, published in 1828, he wrote about the need for difference, and this has become one of the keys to the thinking of Hugo Chávez:

> Spanish America is an original construct. Its institutions and its government must be original as well, and so too must be the methods used to construct them both. Either we shall invent, or we shall wander around and make mistakes.

In April 1825, Rodríguez joined Bolívar on an expedition across the Andes into the newly named country of Bolivia. From Lima, they passed through Arequipa, Cuzco, Tinta, Lampa, Puno and Zepita, and then, once in Bolivia, they travelled on to La Paz, Oruro, Potosí and Chuquisaca (later to be called Sucre, after the victor at Ayacucho).

Bolívar decided that the country to which his name had been given was a place that would benefit from the talents of Rodríguez. He appointed him to be the 'Director of Public Education and Director-General of Mines, Agriculture and Public Roads'. The two friends then separated – Bolívar returned to Peru, while Rodríguez remained in Bolivia. Rodríguez was soon at work in Chuquisaca on the formation of a technical school for local children, Indians as well as whites. Years later, he outlined the extraordinarily ambitious and far-sighted plans he had tried to implement in Bolivia:

> My project at that time was a well-thought-out scheme designed to colonize America with its own inhabitants. I wanted to avoid what I feared might eventually happen one day; that's to say, the sudden invasion of European immigrants with more knowledge than our own people; this would result in them being enslaved once again, and subjected to a worse tyranny than that of the old Spanish system. I wanted to rehabilitate the indigenous race and to prevent it from being entirely exterminated.

Tragically for Bolivia, the conservative citizens of Chuquisaca rejected the imaginative schemes of Rodríguez out of hand. They had only with reluctance accommodated themselves to republican rule. Soon some of the worst fears of Rodríguez were to be realized. The old land-owning class remained in place, and summoned fresh immigrants from Europe. These took their turn at slaughtering and destroying the indigenous peoples, notably during the rubber boom at the end of the nineteenth century. Rodríguez's revolutionary project might have changed the subsequent history of Bolivia, but it was not to be.

Even in Venezuela, the authorities encouraged white immigration from Europe on a huge scale, long before the white settlers had come to terms with the country's aboriginal inhabitants. More than a million European immigrants came to Venezuela after the end of the Second World War in 1945.

Rodríguez set up his school in Chuquisaca and then left on a trip to Cochabamba, where he hoped to establish a new school on the same model. His passion for the education of the Indians was deeply rooted in his appreciation, almost unique at that time, of the role that the underclass played in the country's development. He wrote in 1830 of the debt that could never be repaid:

The scholars of America have never revealed the fact that they owe their knowledge to the Indians and the blacks; for if these scholars had had to plough and sow and reap, and to gather up and prepare everything that they eat and wear and use and play with during their valueless lives, they would not know so much . . .

They would have been working in the fields, and would have been just as brutish as their slaves; they would have been working with them in the mines, in the fields behind the oxen, and on the roads behind the mules, in the stone quarries, and at hundreds of tiny workshops where they make ponchos and coats, and ropes, and shoes and cooking pots.

Rodríguez knew of the hostility of the whites; he had met it 30 years before, in his school in Caracas in the 1790s. Now it was to affect him again. When he returned to Chuquisaca from Cochabamba, he found that his school had been closed down on the orders of the Bolivian president, Antonio José de Sucre y Alcala, one of Bolívar's generals from Venezuela.

Sucre complained that Rodríguez was a hopeless organizer and had failed to keep his school within budget. This may certainly have been true. But the real cause of the closure was the racist attitudes of the Chuquisaca authorities and of the white parents who did not like their children to be educated with Indians. Rodríguez explained later what had happened to the school:

A lawyer named Calvo destroyed my establishment in Chuquisaca, saying that I had exhausted the treasury in order to maintain whores and thieves, instead of devoting my efforts to giving a polish to decent folk.

The whores and the thieves were the children of the real owners of the country, that is, the *cholitos* and *cholitas* who used to run around in the streets and would by now have been considerably more 'decent' than the boys and girls of Señor Calvo.

Depressed by the reception he had received, Rodríguez resigned all his posts in Bolivia and retreated to Peru, perhaps in search of Bolívar. The two men never met again, and there is some suggestion that letters written by Rodríguez to Bolívar never got through to the Liberator. For some years, he sustained himself, and the Bolivian *cholita* he had made his wife, by establishing a candle factory in Ecuador.

Then, in 1834, perhaps summoned by Andrés Bello, he left Ecuador for Chile. He lived and worked for many years in Concepción, and later in Valparaiso. There he set up technical schools, where he taught his pupils to read and write, and then showed them how to make bricks and tiles, and candles. Learning through doing. He is often remembered for causing a scandal by his method of teaching anatomy. Since there were no spare corpses, he would appear naked in the classroom.

After ten years in Chile, he returned, in 1843, to Ecuador, living in the small town of Latacunga. There, in 1847, he set down his views on labour and trade:

> The division of labour in the production of goods only serves to brutalize the workforce. If to produce cheap and excellent nail scissors, we have to reduce the workers to machines, we would do better to cut our finger nails with our teeth.

Rodríguez died in 1852. The year before his death, he wrote of his belief in the desirability of an agrarian revolution:

> If the [Latin] Americans would like the political revolution that the weight of events has created, and whose survival the force of circumstance has permitted, to bring genuine benefits, they must make a genuine economic revolution and they must start in the rural areas: from there the revolution should move on to the industrial workshops. In this way, daily improvements will be observed that could never have been obtained if a start had been made in the cities.

Rodríguez had one further thought:

The Americans must conquer their reluctance to join together to achieve something, and their fear of seeking advice before moving forward. He who does nothing will never make mistakes; yet it is far better to wander around and make mistakes than to go to sleep.

It is not difficult to see why a revolutionary like Hugo Chávez, anxious to revive a nationalist discourse in the age of globalization, should have wished to resurrect the life and writings of this extraordinary man. Simón Bolivar, one of Chávez's other heroes, was much in debt to the old friend he called Samuel Robinson. And so are we all today.

12

EZEQUIEL ZAMORA INVOKES
'HORRÓR A LA OLIGARQUÍA'

Ten milking cows to be farmed out by the landowners on common land, to provide free milk each day to the homes of the poor.
Ezequiel Zamora's plan for the peasantry, *c*.1859

The third exemplary figure recovered by Hugo Chávez from the troubled history of Venezuela in the nineteenth century is that of Ezequiel Zamora, leader of the federal forces in the civil wars of the 1840s and 1850s. Zamora was a provincial radical, a trader who became a soldier and a strategist. He had a far-reaching programme of land reform for the benefit of the peasants, a passionate hostility to the land-owning oligarchy, a project for combining soldiers and civilians in his struggles, and a desire to fulfil the Bolivarian dream of uniting his troops with like-minded forces across the border in Colombia. The aims of this nineteenth-century revolutionary all fit neatly into Chávez's own programme.

Zamora has sometimes been claimed by the left in Venezuela as an early socialist. There is some evidence to suggest that this charismatic soldier, this 'General of the Sovereign People' who was originally a provincial storekeeper, acquired considerable knowledge of the revolutionary upheavals in Europe in his time through his brother-in-law, Juan Gaspers, an immigrant from Alsace. Zamora was certainly familiar with the slogan of 'liberty, equality and fraternity', which he used from time to time, and he was well informed about the European events of 1848. Socialist or not, he was unquestionably a progressive liberal, and a man with advanced opinions for his time and place.

Like Douglas Bravo and the guerrilla movements of the 1960s, who named one of their guerrilla fronts in honour of Zamora, Chávez had long been attracted to Zamora's radical programme, and would discuss it during his lectures at the military college in Caracas in the 1980s. He had been familiar with the story since childhood, for the final campaign of the soldier-revolutionary in 1859 was fought across the territory of his home state of Barinas.

Little survives in writing of Zamora's ideas, but oral traditions collected by Chávez personally, when stationed at Elorza in the *llanos*, sustain the received wisdom that this was a man with a strong sense of solidarity with the rural poor. His appeal to the insurgent peasantry was based on three slogans, often recalled by Chávez:

Tierra y hombres libres; Land and free men;
Elección popular; General elections;
¡Horrór a la oligarquía! Hatred of the oligarchy!

For many years after his death, and after the victory of his conservative opponents, the name of Zamora was held in low esteem. The local oligarchy, says Chávez, never forgave Zamora for the action that he took against their interests when he sacked the town of Barinas. He ordered that the building holding the archives of the land titles should be burnt to the ground. In an action reminiscent of the French Revolution, he wanted the land seizures of the peasants to be freed from retrospective legal action by the land-owners.

Rómulo Gallegos, writer and once briefly the president of Acción Democrática, muddied the republican waters by comparing him with José Tomás Boves (1782–1814), the uncompromising leader of the *llaneros*, the cowboys of the Orinoco, who fought with the Spanish royalists against Bolívar in 1814, and captured Caracas from the republicans. In his novel, *Pobre Negro*, published in 1937, Gallegos describes how Zamora had once been welcomed by the village crowds:

'It is Boves who is coming back, said the old men, and he now calls himself Ezequiel Zamora. Like Boves, he knows how to sweep the people along with him . . .'

The strength of Boves lay in his capacity to mobilize the oppressed classes, the slaves and the Indians, against the republicans. 'From the start of his campaign,' wrote José Ambrosio Llamozas in 1815, 'he revealed the nature of the strategy he was following and from which he never diverted: it was based on the destruction of all the whites, while rescuing and preserving and flattering the coloureds . . . The houses and the goods of those who were killed or exiled would be handed out to the *pardos*, who would also receive title to the land.'

This was *horrór* to the *oligarquía* indeed! When Boves finally captured republican Caracas in July 1814, he destroyed the town, forcing Bolívar to escape into exile in Jamaica. Boves did not long survive, for he was killed later in the year.

Zamora was a popular leader, and he certainly proclaimed 'hatred of the oligarchy', but there is no evidence that he mounted the kind of uncompromisingly racist campaign favoured by the *llanero* cowboy. Yet he certainly bequeathed a conflictive legacy. The state of Barinas was once known as Zamora state, but it was later renamed by local landlord politicians who disliked seeing Zamora commemorated in this way. Zamora's statue in the Plaza Zamora in Barinas was taken down and thrown into the San Domingo river that runs alongside the square.

All this was part of the family history of Chávez. He recalls that in 1960, at the age of six, he used to listen to the stories told him by his grandmother, Rosa Chávez, in her house in Sabaneta. She in turn would remember the stories that she had been told in the 1920s by her grandfather, a man who had accompanied Zamora on his march through Barinas in 1859. Here, at Santa Inés, Zamora had secured his greatest victory. Outside Sabaneta, Zamora had crossed the river Bocono by a ford, and here the youthful Chávez would go with his father to fish and to swim. Sometimes he would go with his schoolfriends to the battlefield of Santa Inés itself, always in the hope of finding old bayonets in the sand.

The battle of Santa Inés was Zamora's 'masterpiece', writes Malcolm Deas, an historian at Oxford, 'an elaborate affair of entrenched ambuscades'. Deas argues that Zamora's 'reputation as an egalitarian reformer rests on little more than an extraordinary *don de gente*, a gift for getting on with all classes, just as his military ascendancy came entirely from ability in the field'. Yet there is no doubt that Chávez is right to claim Zamora as a visionary radical who kept the needs of the peasants at the heart of his programme for transforming the country's rural economy. Among his specific proposals to have survived is his four-point plan for the peasantry:

1. the five leagues around each village or town, at all points of the compass, to be set aside for common use;
2. the system of assessing rents on agricultural land to be abolished;
3. the wages of labourers to be fixed in accordance with their work;
4. ten milking cows to be farmed out by the land-owners on common land, to provide free milk each day to the homes of the poor.

Whatever the specific proposals in his programme, Zamora has remained in popular legend as one of Venezuela's most dashing leaders of the nineteenth century. He was not as bloodthirsty as Boves, but he had a similar capacity to mobilize people for action, as indeed does Chávez.

Zamora was born in Cúa, Miranda, in February 1817. His father had died in the wars of independence, and his family moved to Caracas when he was quite young. Zamora subsequently returned to the *llanos*, and earned his living there as a cattle dealer for some years. Later he opened a general store in Villa de Cura.

He became an outspoken supporter of the liberal cause in the epoch of Antonio Leocádio Guzmán (1801–1884), the founder of the Liberal party, and a powerful opponent of the landed oligarchy grouped around the figure of José Antonio Páez (1790–1873), the great long-surviving conservative caudillo who had fought with Bolívar. After a typically fraudulent election in his home town in 1846,

Zamora launched an attack on the forces of the land-owners, allying himself with one of the great native leaders of the *llanos*, 'el indio' José Rangel.

Zamora and Rangel organized the local peasants and slaves into a scratch force, and called it the 'Army of the Sovereign People', but in 1847 they were defeated at the battle of Laguna del Piedra. Zamora and Rangel were captured and sentenced to death. Rangel was killed with blows from a machete, but Zamora was reprieved and given a ten-year prison sentence. Escaping near Maracay on his way to the prison at Maracaibo, he found work as a labourer on a hacienda until he was granted an amnesty the following year.

He then enrolled in the Liberal Army of José Tadeo Monagas (1785–1868), and continued the fight against the land-owners. In 1849, his troops brought the oligarchs' leader, José Antonio Páez, in chains to Caracas, and in 1851 he became the military commander in Coro. In 1854, when the slaves were finally granted their freedom, Zamora campaigned, albeit unsuccessfully, against the provision of compensation to the slave-owners.

The land-owners' defeat was only temporary, and soon they came back, led by President Julián Castro. Zamora and other liberal leaders went into exile in the Caribbean, but in October 1858, a group of exiles formed a 'Patriotic Junta' and planned a rebellion. They were to be led by General Juan Cristóstomo Falcón, whose sister Zamora had married.

Zamora returned to the mainland, making a successful attack on Coro in February 1859. He then began a campaign in the west that lasted until his death, ten months later, at the battle of San Carlos. His greatest success, at Santa Inés in December 1859, caused the government forces led by Pedro Ramos to retreat to Mérida, leaving the states of Coro, Barinas and Portuguesa in the hands of the federal forces.

Chávez frequently refers to the battle of Santa Inés in his speeches (and he was thrilled to discover on a visit to Havana that the omniscient Fidel Castro knew all about it). When urging the citizens to vote 'yes' in the referendum campaign for the new constitution, held on 15 December 1999, Chávez made a speech describing the battle ahead, and compared his own position with that of Zamora:

> At the battle of Santa Inés, Zamora pretended that his troops were retreating, allowing those of the 'no' camp to advance and to take Barinas without firing a shot. Zamora, from the 'yes' camp, had prepared an ambush, launched a counter-attack, and hit them with a terrific blow, pursuing them as far as Mérida.

Chávez's aim was to repeat Zamora's success at the referendum.

Chávez also claims Zamora as a link in the chain that connects the project of Bolívar with the programme that Chávez wishes to pursue. Zamora is seen by Chávez to be following in the footsteps of Bolívar, pursuing the goal of Latin American unity through an integral alliance with Colombia:

> In Zamora you will find the same Bolívarian geo-political thinking about the unity of Latin America; he had tried to link up his forces with those who were fighting for the Federation in Colombian territory across the Apure river. On 19 May 1859, in a proclamation to the peoples of Barinas and Apure, he described 'the new era of the Colombian Federation that was now opening up, that had been the final wish of our Liberator, the great Bolívar'.

Zamora has one further characteristic that Chávez has invoked. In a painting of Zamora by José Ignacio Chaquett, after the battle of Santa Inés, and one that has sometimes been copied by Chávez, the warrior-hero is depicted in profile wearing two hats, one placed rather unusually on top of the other. One is an ordinary bowler (*sombrero*), the other is a military cap (*képis*). For Zamora, the purpose of his outfit was to symbolize the unity of the people and the armed forces in their efforts 'to make the Revolution'. In his aim of restructuring the relationship between civil society and the armed forces, Comandante Chávez tries to maintain this tradition.

Zamora's legend survives today in the couplets of a military song from the era of the federal wars. These were written down by and put to music by Domingo Castro, a musician in his army:

El cielo encapatado anuncia tempestad,
Y el sol tras de las nubes pierda su claridad.
¡Oligarcas temblad, viva la libertad!
Las tropas de Zamora al toque de clarín,
Derrotan las brigadas del godo malandrín.
The overcast sky warns of the storm to come,
While the sun behind the clouds loses its bright shine,
¡Oligarchs tremble, long live freedom!
The troops of Zamora, at the bugle's sound,
Will destroy the brigades of the reactionary scoundrels.

In a recent account of Zamora's great battle at Santa Inés, Román Martínez Galindo complains that today's generation of Venezuelan children are overly influenced by television, and television from the United States at that. Martínez laments the fact that they 'are more familiar with "the conquest of the West", "the annexation of Texas", or "the American civil war between the north and the south", than they are with the Federal War in Venezuela'. Zamora's story, he suggests, is 'an episode in our history of singular importance, written by our nearest forebears, which we ought to know about if we really want to know who we are'.

Martínez Galindo expresses the hope that one day 'the talented film-makers of Venezuela will decide to rescue us from the cowboy movies of colonialism, from the Marines and the Green Berets . . . and we shall be able to see the General of the Sovereign People at the cinema, playing his bugle at the front of his troops as they sing: *¡Oligarcas temblad!*'

PART THREE

PREPARING THE OVERTHROW
OF THE ANCIEN RÉGIME

13

YARE PRISON, 1992–1994, AND
THE SEARCH FOR POLITICAL ALLIES

The original projects of [the Movement for Socialism] were social justice, equality, freedom, democracy, and the democratic revolution; those were the slogans that I used to hear when I was a school-boy in Barinas . . .

Hugo Chávez, interviewed in June 1998

For his part in organizing the coup attempt of February 1992, Colonel Chávez was given a long prison sentence. In practice, he was only locked up for two years, from February 1992 to March 1994. Imprisoned first in San Carlos, he was moved later to San Francisco de Yare. He was well treated in prison, and looked after in a manner befitting a distinguished officer. He was allowed to be interviewed for radio and to receive many visitors, some of whom were to play an important role in his political formation, and later in his government. He also had time to read and to think, and to consider more fully the nationalist foundations of his political philosophy.

While Chávez was still in prison, a number of dramatic events took place on the national stage. President Carlos Andrés Pérez, who had survived the two military coups of 1992, was finally removed from power in June 1993 by what was, in effect, a congressional coup. He had lost the support of the old guard in Acción Democrática, his own party. Ganging up against him in Congress, they accused him of corruption, and, with two of his ministers, he was forced to resign from office. He was replaced for what was left of his term by Ramón J. Velásquez, a distinguished historian.

When fresh presidential elections were held in December 1993, Colonel Chávez called on his supporters to abstain, and many of them did so. The voting pattern was of little comfort to the established parties. When Pérez had been elected in December 1988, a quarter of the potential voters had abstained. In December 1993, the abstention rate had risen to 40 per cent, a rather larger percentage of the electorate than the miserable 30 per cent that actually voted for the eventual winner, former president Rafael Caldera.

The political strength of the old parties was crumbling. The economic crisis, the *Caracazo*, the two attempted coups d'etat and their own internal dissensions were paving the way for catastrophe. Almost for the first time in Venezuelan politics, the four principal candidates received a similar slice of the vote. Claudio Fermín for Acción Democrática received 23.60 per cent, Oswaldo Alvarez Paz for Copei received 22.73 per cent, and Andrés Velásquez for La Causa R received 21.95 per cent. Only Caldera, with 30 per cent, managed to edge ahead, and everyone recognized that he owed his victory to his famous speech to Congress in February 1992, in which he virtually legitimized the Chávez coup. By innate political skill or by simple good fortune, Caldera had conducted his campaign as an independent, forming a group called Convergencia which was allied with the Movimiento al Socialismo (MAS). Once the founder of Copei, he had abandoned his old party, and they had abandoned him.

Although Caldera was the winner by a short head, he did not have anything ressembling a majority in Congress. His government was hamstrung from the start, and he was obliged to beg for support from Luís Alfaro Ucero, the leader of Acción Democrática.

Political scientists began to talk for the first time in terms of the 'messianic' nature of Venezuela's political culture. Caldera was seen as the magician of the moment, rather as Pérez had been in 1988. Caldera was the man who might put the country back together again, against all the odds, Later in the 1990s, so desperate had the political situation become, miracle candidates appeared on all sides. One was to be Irene Sáez, the former beauty queen who became mayor of Chacao. Another was to be Colonel Chávez.

New forces were now emerging in the country. One important feature of the election of 1993 was the large vote of La Causa R, the radical workers' party in Bolívar state, which had already had some influence on Chávez. This now became the third largest force in the country after the two main parties. The two largest parties together received fewer votes than the two smaller, and more recent, configurations, Caldera's Convergencia (which included the Movement to Socialism) and La Causa R.

The two left-wing parties were now significant players on the national stage. The Movement to Socialism decided to jump in with Caldera, while La Causa R decided to wait awhile. Both were eventually, after serious splits, to support Chávez.

The Movement to Socialism is a small but intellectually significant political organization that has followed most of the ups and downs of comparable socialist movements in Europe, oscillating between 'euro-communism' and social democracy. A large proportion of the intellectual left in Venezuela has moved in or out of MAS during its 30-year existence, and its fierce internal dissensions have provided most of the raw material for what passes in Venezuela for political debate.

Established early in the 1970s by former members of the Communist Party, some of whom had fought in the guerrilla movements of the 1960s, its most articulate spokesman, and several times presidential candidate, was Teodoro Petkoff. Disenchanted with the guerrilla struggle, and disillusioned by the Soviet invasion of Czechoslovakia in 1968, Petkoff's political trajectory has been a slow slide to the right, though his actions have always been informed by a strong moral sense of what it is right to do at any given moment. During the crisis of the 1990s, he perceived it as his job to steer the MAS towards the support of Rafael Caldera's rather abject minority government.

Petkoff himself played a key role in that government as the minister of planning, pushing through a number of neo-liberal reforms. He was joined in the government by another well-known former Communist and MAS supporter, Pompeyo Márquez, who became Caldera's minister for frontiers.

Acknowledging his political debt to Colonel Chávez, which had given him the edge over the other candidates, President Caldera gave orders early in his presidency for those involved in the two military coups in 1992 to be released. Chávez came out of prison on Palm Sunday, 27 March 1994.

During his time in prison, Chávez, like Caldera, had been looking around for political allies. He had renewed his contacts with a number of civilian figures he had encountered before the coup. Luís Miquilena was a frequent visitor, of course, as well as others from the Patriotic Front formed in 1989. He talked to people from the MAS and from La Causa R, but he seems to have drawn the line at Bandera Roja (Red Flag), a *groupuscule* that still championed the armed struggle and had some claim to be an heir to the guerrillas of the 1960s. Chávez never had much time for the ultra-left:

> Groups like them appear to have given themselves the holy mission of proclaiming themselves to be the only revolutionaries on the planet, or at any rate in this territory. And those who don't follow their dogmas are not considered genuine revolutionaries. I have never talked for more than five minutes with a single leader of Bandera Roja.

Although Teodoro Petkoff was working with Caldera, another prominent figure in the MAS, Jorge Giordani, had been a regular visitor to the prison at Yare. A development economist trained at the University of Sussex, and a professor at the Universidad Central in Caracas and at Cendes, Giordani was the economic guru of the MAS. He had refused to support the Caldera government and he was now to become one of Chávez's principal economic advisers. Many of the half-formulated economic ideas of Chávez come from his interaction with Giordani, who in 1999 was appointed minister of development in the Chávez government in charge of Cordiplan.

The MAS was not synonymous with Petkoff by any means, and when the possibility of a Chávez presidency emerged above the horizon in 1998, Giordani and a majority of the MAS eventually chose to support Chávez. Petkoff was still a minister in Caldera's government, and had no desire to jump ship. He was also clearly in complete disagreement with the political proposals of Chávez in almost every sphere. But the rest of his party signed up with Chávez.

When asked why MAS had supported his presidential bid, Chávez noted that the leadership had been rather reluctant, but had been put under pressure by the rank and file. Interviewed by Agustín Blanco Muñoz on 24 June 1998, he said he thought that the membership had probably supported him for quite a long time:

> When I came out of prison at Yare, during the extensive journeys that I made through the country, the people from the MAS were always there, always hoping to talk. I'm sure that most of the political base of the MAS, the political structure that exists all over the country, were always on our side, and had never agreed with the strategy of supporting the [Caldera] government, and even less with the subsequent decisions taken by the leadership . . . I think that they were able to put sufficient pressure on the leaders of the party to enable them to make a decision that was more in line with the party's roots: its original projects of social justice, equality, freedom, democracy, and the democratic revolution. Those were the slogans that I used to hear when I was a schoolboy in Barinas at the time when the MAS was born. That was about the same year, in 1971, that I joined the army.

Chávez made the acquaintance of another intriguing political operative in these years, an historian from Argentina called Norberto Ceresole. A man with roots on the left, Ceresole had subsequently moved to positions more closely identified with the right, and Chávez's early connections with Ceresole have often been cited to indicate the reactionary nature of his views.

Ceresole claims to have been a member in the 1970s of the Montoneros, the Peronist guerrilla group that sprang to prominence during the government of Perón in the 1970s and that of his widow, Isabel. Subsequently he was to argue in favour of the military coup against President Isabel Perón in 1976 by General Jorge Videla, and to claim that the human rights organizations that criticized the excesses of Argentina's 'dirty war' were part of a 'Jewish plot' against the nation. Ceresole was also the author of many books. One of them, *La Conquista del Imperio Americano*, published by Al-Andalus in Madrid in 1998, contains a powerful denunciation of 'the Jewish financial mafia' behind American capitalism.

Ceresole was undoubtedly useful to Chávez at this early stage because of his well-established historical interest in 'progressive' military governments. As a radical Peronist, Ceresole looked back to Nasser and Ataturk, and he had also written books in support of the Peruvian General Velasco and the Panamanian General Torríjos. Ceresole had a number of connections with Arab governments which were to prove extremely useful. Yet a continuing friendship with this controversial Argentinian might have proved embarrassing, and when Chávez became president, Ceresole was conveniently spirited out of the country, and he returned to Buenos Aires.

14

LA CAUSA R, PATRIA PARA TODOS AND POLITICS IN GUAYANA

> La Causa R rejected a strategy of sustaining the mega-projects
> involved in the export-oriented industry of primary products . . .
> and concentrated instead . . . on medium-scale manufacturing
> industry that would transform raw materials within Bolívar state
> itself.
>
> Margarita López Maya

Ciudad Bolívar, once called Angostura because of the narrowness of the river, is a tiny colonial town perched high above the Orinoco on its southern shore. A tree-girt walk borders the river, with railings to prevent anyone falling victim to the crocodiles that were once such a feature of this strategic waterway. Walter Raleigh came here, to Angostura, and so too did the German scientist and traveller Alexander von Humboldt, recovering for several weeks after a bout of fever.

Simón Bolívar was also based at Angostura, in the years before the town was renamed in his honour. He came here first in 1816 before his dramatic advance through the Andean passes to Colombia. Then, in 1819, the congress that he had assembled from the liberated peoples of the lands of the Orinoco and the shores of the Caribbean appointed him to be the president and military commander of the new state of Gran Colombia.

'Fortunate the citizen,' said Bolívar at the opening of the Angostura Congress, 'who, under the protection of arms, calls on national sovereignty to exercise its unrestricted will.' President Chávez was to quote the same words when he summoned a new National Assembly to draft a new constitution 180 years later, in 1999.

Angostura, or Ciudad Bolívar as it now is, was once an important trading centre but today basks in the glory of its forgotten history. It still retains some significance as the capital of Bolívar state and as the gateway to the plains of the lower Orinoco and the eastern region of Guayana. Beyond the town, a great motorway leads on to Ciudad Guayana, the centre of Venezuela's largest planned industrial complex, an area with an heroic, pioneering feel, reminiscent of the Soviet Union in its heyday. This is the power house of Venezuela, a place where the state assumed responsibility for the development of heavy industry and for the energy provisions once deemed necessary for a modern economy.

You might think that because Venezuela has so much oil it would have been content to build oil-fired power stations. But this is not so. Ambitious governments long ago decided to sell oil on the foreign market and to develop hydro-electric power at home for local industry. The Guayana region now contains the second largest hydro-electric complex in the world, on the Caroní river at Guri. Only the Itaipú dam on the Paraná river, on the border between Brazil and Paraguay, is larger. Here too are the excavations of the immense iron mountain of Cerro Bolívar, the huge steel works run by Siderúrgica del Orinoco (Sidor), and the embryonic aluminium industry. All these were set up and run by the all-powerful state.

To serve and manage these gigantic enterprises has required a huge labour force, attracted to the region from all over the country, and not surprisingly, the region has become famous for its radical politics. A powerful workers' movement, independent of the unions of the previous governments and developed over a period of 30 years now furnishes President Chávez with strong support.

Ciudad Guayana is the birthplace of La Causa R, a political organization that is unique to Venezuela. Originally set up in the early 1970s, La Causa R, or Radical Cause, developed in 1997 into Patria Para Todos (PPT), the Fatherland for Everyone, now an integral part of Chávez's governing coalition, the Polo Patriótico. The PPT provides the government with several of its most important ministers, and many of its most lucid ideas.

La Causa R was founded in the 1970s by Alfredo Maneiro, a guerrilla fighter of the Communist Party in the previous decade. Maneiro's group, like the Movimiento al Socialismo of Teodoro Petkoff, had split away from the old Venezuelan Communist Party in 1970 at the end of the guerrilla war. Maneiro, born in 1939, had been a member of the central committee of the Communist Party, and a guerrilla commander on the eastern front. When the Communist Party splintered in the late 1960s, he was close to the Chinese position in the Sino-Soviet dispute, an attitude radically different from that of dissidents like Petkoff who were moving towards European-style social democracy. One of Maneiro's disciples was Pablo Medina, once a labour organizer, now an important and prominent civilian supporter of Hugo Chávez, and a member of the Constituent Assembly in 1999.

Maneiro's group participated in the formation of MAS in January 1971, but it soon moved off in a new direction. Maneiro had been highly critical of the old Communist Party of the 1960s, and not just because of its ideology. He began to question the desirability of political parties themselves, and soon he had formulated an ideological position hostile to these organizational constructs. In a collection of articles, *Notas Negativas*, published in 1971, he outlined the political position of a new left-wing nationalist group he called 'Venezuela 83'. It was to be the forerunner of the party known as La Causa R.

The figure '83' was a reference to the year 1983. At that time, then more than ten years distant, the foreign oil companies operating in Venezuela, would, according to the terms of a treaty signed in 1944, be required to hand over their concessions to the Venezuelan state. This was an event to which Venezuelan nationalist opinion looked forward with keen anticipation. (In practice, Carlos Andrés Pérez, ever the populist demagogue, was able to advance the date to 1976, the year when the oil companies were finally nationalized.)

Maneiro's political aim – a highly original one – was to canalize the protest movements of the people without the creation of a party political structure. The historian Margarita López Maya has described his project:

> He said it was necessary both to create a political framework for the extraordinary and spontaneous mobilizing capacity of the masses, and to participate in the infinite and varied forms of a popular movement; but this had to be done in the firm belief that the masses themselves would decide on their own political direction. Instead of starting with a given political structure, it was important to trust in the capacity of the popular movement to take on the task of producing a new leadership from within its ranks.

With this interesting and innovative political philosophy formulated and in place, Maneiro and his group decided to concentrate on three particular areas of popular mobilization where the necessary vanguard leadership might eventually emerge. One was the student movement based at the Universidad Central in Caracas, an effervescent political organization housed in the magnificent modernist buildings of Carlos Raúl Villanueva. With strong roots dating back over the generations to 1918, 1928 and 1958, as well as to 1968, the university had been associated for many years with the left. A second area of popular protest was the western Caracas suburb of Catia, with a mixed population of half a million people and considerable traditions of popular struggle.

Political activity on both these fronts – in the university and in Catia – was initially successful but eventually proved politically unrewarding. La Causa R concentrated its efforts on the third area chosen by Maneiro, the workers' movement in Ciudad Guayana associated with the state steel industry, Sidor. A long strike there had left the workers highly politicized and critical of the government unions that

POLITICS IN GUAYANA 137

were controlled by Acción Democrática. Here the Maneiro philosophy was tested and found to be satisfactory.

The great public works of Ciudad Guayana – the Sidor steel works and the great dams on the Caroní river – were the fruit of decisions taken much earlier, in the era of the last military dictator, General Pérez Jiménez, in the 1950s. Pérez Jiménez, a figure that everyone has preferred to forget, still lives, at a great age, in exiled retirement in Spain. In the Miraflores Palace in Caracas, a row of presidential portraits moves seamlessly from Rómulo Gallegos (overthrown in 1948) to Rómulo Betancourt (who took power in 1958). Pérez Jiménez, who ruled in the ten years in between, has become a nonperson, removed from history. Yet he took many of the fundamental decisions that were to affect the Venezuelan economy for fifty years, decisions of such dimension and implication that no subsequent president ever had the courage or the opportunity to reappraise them until the 1990s.

Luís Miquilena, Chávez's most prominent political adviser, has an interestingly ambivalent attitude towards the dictatorship of Pérez Jiménez. Although a victim of the repression at that time, Miquilena now has a rather appreciative view of the achievements of the dictator:

The dictatorship had a rather more developed idea of what the country could be than the supporters of Acción Democrática had at that time. Pérez Jiménez established the foundations of our development – and I can say that with the authority of someone who was imprisoned for seven years during his rule.

During that time, the steel industry was developed, and the principal roads in the country were laid down, indeed there was a plan and a concept of what the country ought to be that had never existed before.

These ideas, says Miquilena, were important, and they were only recovered 'when Chávez presented the idea of establishing a new country by taking the democratic road'.

Venezuela's industrial development, envisaged by the Pérez Jiménez government, should have been a straightforward task. With cheap iron and bauxite, cheap electricity and cheap transport on the Orinoco (as well as the proximity of a large market in the United States), the way forward appeared simple and attractive. Yet the state enterprises of Ciudad Guayana were to become the cause of endless economic headaches to successive governments, and, as with the Soviet Union, the disadvantages of state capitalism became increasingly apparent over the years.

The powerful state development agency in the area, the Corporación Venézolana de Guayana (CVG), became a state within a state, corrupt and bureaucratized. Industrial development had been financed from the rent from oil, but when the oil price collapsed in the 1980s, the economic ruin of the Guayana region became increasingly apparent.

On the surface, everything remained much the same. Great motorways plunged across the land, the vast steel works at Sidor remained hard at work, the pharaonic construction of the Guri dam was in full functioning order. Yet an examination of the books revealed the extent of the ruin. Money from oil revenues was channelled through to the political party in power in the region – in league with the unions (themselves a branch of a political party) – permitting gross overmanning. Huge debts were incurred without any thought as to how they might be paid off. Sidor employed 6,000 more men than was economically justifiable. The hydro-electric plant at the Guri dam could not survive if it did not charge an economic price for the electricity it was producing. Other industrial plants required substantial fresh investment, and little was now available from the state. New money would have to come from the foreign investor, and that in turn would demand greater efficiency and more competition – a sea change for state-coddled Venezuela.

Suddenly the workers of the region began listening to the spokesmen of La Causa R. Pablo Medina, another supporter of the guerrillas of the 1960s, had been sent to Sidor as an infiltrated worker years before, in January 1972. The climate for political activity appeared propitious. The new city of Ciudad Guayana had become a magnet for unorganized migrant workers from all over the country, and the growth potential of a creative union organization was rapidly made evident. Medina worked at the steel works on the night shift; during the day he produced a paper, *El Matancero*, highly critical of the dominant Acción Democrática union.

The account of these early activities by Margarita López Maya describes how Medina's paper moved into areas of political struggle that had previously been neglected:

> *El Matancero* battled against the corruption of traditional unionism, and it also fought for the right of workers to democratic participation in union decisions that affected them – something previously unknown in the region – as well as in decisions concerning conditions and safety at the work-place – subjects never touched by other union leaders.

An early recruit to the cause, fulfilling Maneiro's ambition that a new leadership should arise from specific struggles, was Andrés Velázquez, a skilled electrician who was later to become a presidential candidate of the left. In 1977, after five years of sustained political activity, another recruit, Tello Benítez, secured an elected position in the steelworkers' union Sutiss, the Sindicato Unico de los Trabajadores de la Industria Siderúrgica y Similares.

After nearly a decade of political work, the activists associated with *El Matancero* made a momentary breakthrough. At union elections in 1979, the Matancero slate, headed by Velásquez, won a controlling stake in the Sutiss union. It was a pyrrhic victory. Two years later, in 1981, Sutiss was taken over by its parent federation, Fetrametal, an organization controlled by Acción Democrática. Velásquez and Benítez both lost their jobs at the steel works. La Causa R was now at a low ebb, and soon its founding father was gone. Alfredo Maneiro died in November 1982 at the early age of 45.

Several more years elapsed before Sutiss was able to regain its independence, and the Matancero slate won again in 1988. The tide

was turning, and La Causa R came for the first time to national prominence. In the congressional elections of 1988, three LCR candidates
for deputy were successful. The following year, the year of the *Caracazo*, Andrés Velásquez was elected as the governor of Bolívar state in
December 1989. Three years later, in December 1992, he won again,
and another LCR activist, Aristóbulo Isturiz, a prominent figure in the
teachers' union who had given veiled support to the Chávez coup, was
elected mayor of Caracas. Finally, in the presidential elections of
December 1993, Velásquez won 22 per cent of the national vote. It
was an extraordinary triumph.

The programme of Velásquez in 1990 provides some indication of
the national ambitions of La Causa R at that time, and it also gives a
flavour of the ideas that were later to inform the government of Hugo
Chávez.

According to the account by Margarita López Maya, the programme of Velásquez had four principal guidelines: the practice of
democracy was to be understood not just in terms of elections, but in
the actions of government itself; corruption was to be rooted out; and
in the provision of services, especially in health, education and social
security, competence and transparency were to be secured.

The fourth guideline, which referred specifically to the development of the Guayana region, was to outline criteria rather different
from that conceived at the time by the Venezuelan state:

La Causa R rejected a strategy of sustaining the mega-projects
involved in the export-oriented industry of primary products
(iron, aluminium, and bauxite); and aimed instead on the down-
stream activities on the Orinoco, concentrating on medium-scale
manufacturing industry that would transform raw materials
within Bolívar state itself.

There were to be no more mega projects for which the state could
no longer guarantee financing, and a lot more medium-scale enterprises that could be locally sustained. This is the intellectual legacy

that La Causa R has bequeathed to the government of Hugo Chávez. Some writers have suggested that La Causa R, with its emphasis on workers and on unionism, bears some resemblance to the Partido de los Trabalhadores of Lula in Brazil. In practice, a more satisfactory parallel is with the Green parties in Europe, particularly in Germany. La Causa R is not in any way a traditional leftist party.

In the aftermath of the Chávez coup of 1992, La Causa R secured one of its most prominent recruits, Colonel Francisco Arias Cárdenas, the companion of Chávez in the Bolivarian Revolutionary Movement and the officer who seized Maracaibo during the coup attempt. Arias was a native of the state of Zulia, and in the elections for state governors in 1996 he was elected to his home state as the candidate of La Causa R.

This was probably the high point of what had once been Maneiro's organization. La Causa R subsequently became swamped by the spring tide of the Chávez phenomenon. Like all political movements in Venezuela, it was confronted with unexpected decisions. Should it support Chávez for president or reject him?

In February 1997, La Causa R divided into two different groups: a small rump remained with the name La Causa R while a new and larger organization came into being called Patria Para Todos (PPT), Fatherland for Everyone.

The division brought Andrés Velásquez into conflict with Pablo Medina. Velásquez remained with La Causa R, supported by Ana Brunswick, the widow of Alfredo Maneiro, while Medina, supported by Aristóbulo Istúriz, Ali Rodríguez Araque and Alberto Müller Rojas, formed the PPT and threw their weight behind the presidential campaign of Hugo Chávez.

The PPT became an important component of the Polo Patriótico alliance created to support the presidential bid of Hugo Chávez in 1998. At least four of its members play influential roles in the Chávez government. One of them is Colonel Arias Cárdenas, the governor of Zulia. Another is Ali Rodríguez Araque, a former guerrilla comandante of the 1960s who became the minister of energy and mines in

1999, and who is now the man behind the new dynamic policy towards Opec. Yet another is Aristóbulo Istúriz, the vice-president of the Constituent Assembly. Pablo Medina is the PPT's secretary-general, while Alberto Müller Rojas is Chávez's ambassador in Santiago de Chile.

15

THE PRESIDENTIAL
ELECTION OF 1998

The fight for power in Venezuela, said Chávez in April 1997, would be between two poles: the 'patriotic pole' led by the Bolivarian Revolutionary Movement, and the 'pole of national destruction' led by the old political parties.

Once out of prison in March 1994, Colonel Chávez began to consider his political future. Initially, he remained opposed to participating in elections. The old system was too corrupt, and too weighted against newcomers. He concentrated at first on publicizing the two principal items on his political agenda: the need to dissolve the Congress, and the need to summon a constituent assembly to draft a new constitution.

Chávez's rejection of the existing political system was so rooted that he opposed the candidature of his friend and colleague, Francisco Arias Cárdenas, as governor of Zulia in 1995. Arias was not supported by the Bolivarian Revolutionary Movement (MBR-200), as he might have expected to be, but by La Causa R.

Early in 1997, Chávez's outlook began to change. His popular support was growing, and his conversations with La Causa R and with the Movimiento al Socialismo were prospering. Looking forward to the presidential elections of 1998, he had just two years in which to transform this support into an organization capable of mounting an election campaign – and winning it. By July 1998, six months before the election, he had secured 45 per cent in the polls.

First he began to reconstruct his Bolivarian Revolutionary Movement into a proper political organization, with both military and civilian support. He announced in January 1997 that his Movement would be in power 'before the year 2000', and in April he formally declared his intention to stand for the presidency.

The Movement held its first congress that month, and the delegates decided that they should field candidates in all the elections scheduled for December 1998. Elections were to be held at the same time for president and Congress, and for state governors and local mayors. The fight for power in Venezuela, Chávez told the delegates, would be between two poles: the 'patriotic pole' led by the Bolivarian Movement, and the 'pole of national destruction' led by the old political parties.

For a number of reasons, the Bolivarian Movement – which included serving as well as retired officers – seemed an unsuitable vehicle for the preparation of a civilian electoral campaign. There was opposition within the Movement about the electoral strategy. Some members argued that it would lead to an eventual watering down of their radical programme, as had already happened with progressive movements like the Movimiento al Socialismo and La Causa R.

Chávez himself argued that they should not miss the opportunity to campaign when so many elected positions were at stake. But in view of this internal opposition, he decided to keep the Bolivarian Movement as it was and create a new political grouping that could be organized into an electoral force. In July he named his new organization the Movimiento Quinta Republica (MVR), the Fifth Republic Movement. Venezuela needed to create a new republic, he said, and the new movement's name was designed to indicate a complete break with the past.

Venezuela had had four republics since the declaration of independence from Spain in 1811. Two were formed during the wars of independence: the Confederation of the States of Venezuela in 1811, and the Second Republic of 1813; the Third Republic was created at the time of the formation of Gran Colombia in 1819. The Fourth Republic, founded in Valencia in 1830 by Bolívar's general, José Antonio Páez, was to last the longest. Built, said Chávez, by 'a class of oligarchs and bankers, on the bones of Bolívar and Sucre', Venezuela's Fourth Republic had always been dominated by conservatives opposed to the ideals of Bolívar.

Chávez now aimed at founding a Fifth Republic, the first new beginning for 140 years. His movement, he said, would have 'a national and popular character'. It would seek to recover the ideals of the past, and would be founded on the ideas of Bolívar:

> Its mission is to secure the well-being of the national community, to satisfy the individual and collective aspirations of the Venezuelan people, and to guarantee a state of optimum prosperity for the fatherland.

While it is tempting to imagine that Chávez may have been seeking to make a parallel with the changes wrought in France by General Charles de Gaulle after the collapse of the French Fourth Republic in 1958, it may be that for many Venezuelans the idea of a 'Fifth Republic' was not unconnected in their minds with the millenarian notion of the 'Fifth Monarchy'. Certainly the bookstores of Caracas were groaning with 'New Age' material in the last years of the twentieth century, and one book even suggested that Venezuelans were a nation of the elect, specially chosen for the accomplishment of God's purposes.

The 'Fifth Monarchy Men' who were politically active in Britain in the seventeenth century believed that the four monarchies of Babylon, Persia, Greece and Rome would soon be followed by the rule of the Saints. The projected utopia of the Saints would be marked by the abolition of tithes, the reform of the laws, the humbling of the rich and the exaltation of the poor. Chávez's millenarian notion of a new start after the evils and corruption of the past must have struck a chord with the thousands of voters familiar with the language of Protestant preachers and Seventh Day Adventists.

Chiliastic movements have been relatively common in the Third World, and Chávez's campaign must surely have made an appeal to that huge underclass which, in Venezuela as elsewhere in Latin America in recent years, has embraced the Protestant evangelical church in all its different varieties with unusual fervour, and in growing numbers. Several Chávez campaign posters carried religious portraits of the comandante that were indistinguishable from the millenarian pictures distributed by evangelical sects. Since Chávez speaks with the rhetoric of an evangelical preacher, invoking pain and love and redemption, the chiliastic nature of his popular appeal should not be underestimated.

To start with, the new Fifth Republic Movement was quite small. An estimated 60 per cent of the initial membership came from the military participants in the Bolivarian Movement, while about 40 per cent were independent civilians of no fixed ideology.

Early in 1998, the election year, the bandwagon began to roll. Other parties offered their formal support to the Chávez campaign. First on board, in March, was Patria Para Todos, one of the wings of La Causa R. It was followed in May by the Movimiento al Socialismo. Both groups were to split in the process. The MAS lost two of its 'historic' leaders, Teodoro Petkoff and Pompeyo Márquez. The PPT lost its leader in Guayana, Andrés Velásquez.

The new *chavista* alliance, called the Polo Patriótico, effectively drew a line under the history of MAS and La Causa R, the two left-wing parties that had split from the Communist Party in the early 1970s, and slowly built up their strength as independent forces. From now on, their ideas would survive and prosper, to fill the ideological vacuum within Chávez's MVR, which had little to offer beyond its ill-defined nationalism and its chiliastic enthusiasms. Yet at the same time, both MAS and La Causa R had signed the death warrant of their organizations as independent operators. With Chávez firmly in the saddle, seducing more than half the country to accompany him on a journey towards an obviously positive though uncertain destiny, the need for separate political organizations was no longer self-evident. Their important contribution was to have infused the MVR with their particular and differing brands of leftist ideology, much of which was outlined in the development plan that Chávez had published in 1995, called the Bolívarian Alternative Agenda.

In July 1998, the Polo Patriótico began to discuss the crucial questions of a political alliance. How would the individuals within its component parts secure their election to the Congress, or as state governors, at the elections now scheduled for November? Overwhelmed by the need for unity, they overcame their individual party loyalties and it was agreed that the Polo Patriótico would support a single candidate in each state.

As the support for Chávez became ever more firm and united in election year, so the unpopularity of the old political parties became ever more manifest. Indeed the bosses of Acción Democrática and Copei became nervous about putting forward a presidential candidate of their own. Chávez appeared to have a huge advantage as an independent who had come from nowhere, and Copei decided to look for a popular outsider with a chance of defeating Chávez. The obvious candidate was the former beauty queen, Irene Sáez, the successful and innovative mayor of the wealthy Caracas zone of Chacao. Six months before the elections, Irene was given an approval rate in the polls of about 22 per cent. Having no candidate of its own, Copei decided to support her.

It proved a poisoned chalice. A few months later her ratings had slipped to just 2 per cent. She herself was quite popular. Her collapse was entirely due to her mistaken alliance with Copei. Not wholly understanding how much it was disliked, Copei now rapidly abandoned the beauty queen and transferred its support, just weeks before the election, to Henrique Salas Römer, the candidate of the last remaining conservative grouping, called 'Proyecto Venezuela'. At that stage, Salas Römer was registering an approval rating of over 40 per cent, just below Chávez.

Changing candidates in the middle of the campaign, far from rein-forcing the prospects of the chosen figure, merely reduced their chance of victory. To receive the official blessing of Copei was tantamount to receiving a curse against which there was no appeal.

If Copei had behaved shabbily towards Irene Sáez, the perfidy of Acción Democrática was even more striking. Initially, in Luís Alfaro Ucero, they had a candidate of their own, an ancient party warhorse with considerable political skills honed over the years. Yet by Novem-ber 1998, within a month of the election, the party bosses were getting worried. Alfaro's approval rating in the polls was hovering around the 6 per cent mark.

The leadership of the party decided to jump ship. They expelled Alfaro from the party to which he had given a lifetime's service, and they too joined Copei on the life raft provided by the unfortunate Salas Römer. With these two millstones on board, support from the two most unpopular and discredited parties in the country, Salas Römer was lucky to come second on 6 December with 39 per cent. Irene Sáez came third with 4 per cent, and Alfaro Ucero came fourth. Hugo Chávez romped home with over 56 per cent of the vote.

The personal vote for Chávez and the Fifth Republic Movement that he had created was so large that it utterly overwhelmed the con-stituent parties of the Polo Patriótico. They might have provided him with a leg up, and they might yet give him ideas and the outlines of a political programme. But essentially they were no longer necessary. Chávez could operate on his own.

Chávez received 3,673,685 votes at the December election, or 56.20 per cent. Their breakdown, according to the numbers for each of the component parts of his electoral alliance, was as follows:

Movimiento Quinta Republica	2,625,839	40.17%
Movimiento al Socialismo	588,643	9.00%
Patria Para Todos	142,859	2.19%
Partido Comunista de Venezuela	81,979	1.25%
Five other small parties	234,365	3.59%

Chávez was now the dominant personality in Venezuela, the maker and breaker of individual politicians and of political parties. Within four years, he had come from prison to the gates of the presidential palace. The old political system lay in ruins all about him. An entirely new era was about to begin.

PART FOUR

CHÁVEZ IN POWER

16

THE FORMATION OF A
CONSTITUENT ASSEMBLY

Our existing laws are disastrous relics derived from every despotic regime there has ever been, both ancient and modern; let us ensure that this monstrous edifice will collapse and crumble, so that we may construct a temple to justice away from its ruins, and dictate a new Venezuelan legal code under the influence of its sacred inspiration.

Bolívar at the Angostura Congress of 1819

At a formal ceremony in Caracas on 2 February 1999, nearly seven years to the day since his failed military coup, Hugo Chávez assumed the presidential sash in the presence of a number of other Latin American presidents. The immediate aims of his government were clear. He would rewrite the constitution of 1961 and he would integrate the armed forces into the economic and social life of the country through a programme he baptized as 'Plan Bolívar 2000'. His other ambitions remained to be spelt out.

In his first speech as president, he announced that he would immediately sign a decree for a national referendum: the people should decide whether elections should be held for a National Constituent Assembly that would draft a new constitution. As if to escape from the widespread belief that he was a military dictator in the making, President Chávez was anxious from the start to make his every move subject to the will of the people. This was to be a year with an unprecedented number of elections; Chávez campaigners did well in all of them.

In November 1998, there were elections for the Congress. In December 1998, there were presidential elections, in which Chávez won 56.2 per cent of the vote. In April 1999, the referendum was held on the desirability of elections to a putative Constituent Assembly; the 'Yes' campaign received 88 per cent of the vote. In July 1999, elections were held for this Assembly; Chávez supporters, standing as independents, received 119 out of 131 seats, and 91 per cent of the vote. Finally, in December 1999, a second referendum ratified the new constitution drafted by the Assembly: 71 per cent voted 'Yes' and 28 per cent voted 'No'. If Venezuelans ever felt deprived of democratic practice, they were now in receipt of it in abundance, and fresh elections to implement the decisions of the Assembly were scheduled for the year 2000.

An integral part of Chávez's thinking since the 1980s had been the need to rewrite the country's old constitution, and to elect a fresh constituent assembly to undertake this task. He and his supporters understood clearly that this was not a job to be left to the old Congress. A clean break with the past was essential. While the proposal appeared to be a fresh idea, the possibility of revising the old constitution of 1961 had been under consideration for a long time. The crisis of the political system had been brewing for many years, and successive governments had made efforts to address it, and considered the possibility of constitutional changes. A Presidential Commission for the Reform of the State (Copre) had been established as long ago as December 1984, during the Acción Democrática government of President Jaime Lusinchi.

Copre reported on the popular dissatisfaction with Acción Democrática and Copei, and recommended a series of reforms: a fresh approach to electoral funding; the development of internal party democracy; an overhaul of the electoral system; and a project of political decentralization. Lusinche took no action, but Carlos Andrés Pérez dusted down the proposals when he returned to power in 1989. The closed-block system of voting, which had enabled the two main parties to keep a tight control over who got elected, was replaced with a more open arrangement under which voters knew who they were actually voting for. State governors and mayors were now elected by direct and secret vote under a simple plurality system.

The result of this change was a number of victories, at a local level, for minority parties. In elections for state governors in 1989, La Causa R won Bolívar state, and MAS won Aragua. Both parties secured a handful of seats in Congress. In 1992, La Causa R won Caracas, and in the presidential elections of 1993, third parties made a major breakthrough. Yet although welcome in themselves, the reforms had not been able to address the wider problem of the country's generalized political disenchantment, signalled by the high abstention rate.

In the crisis atmosphere after the *Caracazo*, a fresh attempt was made in June 1989 to reform the state by tackling the constitution itself. The left-wing Patriotic Front, set up by Luís Miquilena and others, had been among the first to demand the holding of a Constituent Assembly: the constitution of 1961 should be rewritten to establish 'a new republic'. The Congress embraced the idea, and set up a 'Special Joint Chamber Commission for the Revision of the Constitution'. It was presided over by former president Caldera. Although the proposal had come from the left, the commission was dominated, inevitably, by members of the old parties, Acción Democrática and Copei, who had a majority in the Congress.

The commission's original aim was to produce a number of quick reforms to the existing constitution of 1961, but its meetings dragged on interminably. Then, in the wake of the Chávez coup attempt of February 1992, when the depth of the political crisis was once again understood, the discussions were suddenly speeded up. The issue of a new constitution, and in some quarters the demand for a proper Constituent Assembly to draft it, now came to the front of the political stage. To head off these more extreme demands, the commission finally published a draft reform project at the end of March 1992, and presented it to the Congress for discussion.

The debate over the draft took place over several months, yet it was so acrimonious, and so little consensus emerged, that the attempt was abandoned in August. Two years later, during his own presidential election campaign at the end of 1994, Caldera tried to revive the idea, but he got nowhere. Eventually only Chávez was prepared to put the project of creating a new constitution at the heart of his political project.

In his first year as president, the speed of events was breathtaking. On 19 April 1999, the first referendum took place; and on 25 July, elections were held for the new Constituent Assembly, the majority of the successful candidates being those who enjoyed the support of Chávez. Finally, on 3 August, the freshly elected National Constituent Assembly met for the first time in the hemispherical chamber of the Senate, with Miquilena as president and Aristóbulo Istúriz as vice-president.

On 5 August, the members of the new assembly listened to a lengthy speech from President Chávez telling them to produce a constitution in the shortest possible time. To encourage them in their work, he provided a draft of his own. He then reminded them of Bolívar's words, addressed to the first Venezuelan Congress in Angostura in 1819:

> Our existing laws are disastrous relics derived from every despotic regime there has ever been, both ancient and modern; let us ensure that this monstrous edifice will collapse and crumble, so that we may construct a temple to justice away from its ruins, and dictate a new Venezuelan legal code under the influence of its sacred inspiration.

The plenary sessions of the assembly began on the following morning, with the skilled speakers of the opposition making most of the running: Alberto Franceschi, an old Trotskyist demagogue; Jorge Olavarría, a confused but brilliant journalist and editor who had oscillated across the political spectrum for decades, having once been a prospective presidential candidate for La Causa R, as well as the ambassador in London; Allan Brewer Carias, the doyen of Venezuela's constitutional lawyers, an academic who once had a spell in Cambridge and the man with the reputation of having introduced expensive and unreliable voting machines into Venezuela; and Claudio Fermín, known ubiquitously as 'el negro', the only serious politician of the four, who had been the unsuccessful presidential candidate for Acción Democrática in 1993. The great majority of the assembly looked on, silent and stunned.

A decision was soon made to abandon the plenary sessions and to form 21 specialist commissions with the task of defining and debating the various articles of the new constitution. The assembly was then scheduled to meet again in plenary session two months later. One commission, chaired by Hermann Escarrá, was detailed to deal with requests and suggestions coming in from outside.

One issue remained to be decided: the nature of the relationship between the new Constituent Assembly, elected in July, and the old Congress, with its senate and chamber of deputies, elected the previous November.

The Constituent Assembly was now perceived by most jurists as the country's supreme authority, with all other governing institutions subordinate to it. Both President Chávez and Miquilena, as president of the Assembly, hoped for a period of peaceful coexistence between the old and the new before the ratification by referendum of the new constitution.

But in the middle of August an argument arose over the future of the judiciary. Chávez decreed a 'judicial emergency' on 25 August, and a nine-member commission was appointed with powers to dismiss the Supreme Court. Eight out of the 15 members of the Court supported the emergency decree, but their president, Cecilia Sosa, was bitterly opposed and resigned immediately. She declared that the Court was now dead and that the country's democratic system was in danger.

The old political elite, who were still well represented in Congress, now engineered a confrontation between the Congress and the Assembly. They convened a meeting of the Congress on 27 August, in emergency session, to consider the resignation of Cecilia Sosa. Their decision was considered provocative both by Chávez and by the Constituent Assembly, but when the National Guard tried to prevent the congressmen from entering the parliament building in the centre of Caracas, which was also used by the Assembly, there were violent protests in the streets. The supporters of both sides came to blows.

After tempers cooled, there was a stand-off, and after discussions presided over by Church leaders, the Constituent Assembly allowed the Congress to reconvene on 9 September. The Congress members opposed to the Chávez government, who formed a majority in Congress, agreed that they would not pass laws that would hinder the work of the Assembly.

President Chávez, meanwhile, having wound up the clockwork, sensibly took himself on a long global tour to drum up political and economic support in Asia, visiting Japan and Malaysia, and the People's Republic of China, and returning via Madrid and Paris.

Back in Caracas, he found that the Assembly was on the verge of approving a number of articles with which he was not in agreement, some of which would cause him considerable political embarrassment. Two articles in particular, one referring to the freedom of the press, and the other to 'the right to life' (but apparently giving the green light to abortion), seemed likely to bring down on his head the combined wrath of the international media and the Catholic Church – an unusual but powerful alliance. The Assembly had also rejected his own pet project of renaming the country as 'the Bolivarian Republic of Venezuela', a name change that appeared innocent enough on the surface, but encapsulated in coded form his ambitious plans for the future of Latin America.

One observer, Celina Romero, writing in late September, noted how 'international scrutiny' was beginning to play 'a significant role in the transition process'. Romero examined how 'the beleaguered opposition' was using 'its international ties and the media' to denounce what it perceived as 'the dismantling of the 41-year-old democratic system'.

Chávez refused to accept this blackmail, and he dealt very firmly with the various international groups that descended on the city to complain about what was going on. He was in a difficult situation since he realized that some of the clauses in the new draft of the new constitution might be offensive to certain interest groups; on the other hand, he did not want to interfere overtly in the affairs of the 'sovereign' Assembly. The crisis passed, and the clauses were toned down, and Chávez also managed to have reinstated his desire to rename the country as 'a Bolivarian republic'.

The draft of the eventual constitution was eventually ready in the middle of October. At one stage it appeared to have more than 1,000 articles, but these were gradually whittled down until there were, first, 450, and then, finally, 396. The Assembly members were told that they had just a month in which to meet in plenary session to debate and revise the wording. Working every morning and every afternoon, each day of the week, they finished on 12 November. The document was submitted to a referendum on 15 December.

17

MANUEL QUIJADA AND THE REFORM
OF THE JUDICIARY

Checking through the files . . . the commission discovered that 4,000 complaints had been made in the past ten years against judges and prosecutors.

At the heart of the crisis of the old Venezuelan state lay the corruption of the judiciary. This was a situation that the election of Hugo Chávez was designed to remedy, and which his government was pledged to reform. A 'judicial emergency commission' of the newly elected Constituent Assembly was set up in August to draft the legal clauses of the new constitution, to examine the state of the existing provisions, and to evaluate the work both of judges and of the members of the Supreme Court.

The new commission was presided over by Manuel Quijada, a lawyer and a strong Chávez supporter, who had been a member of the Patriotic Front set up in 1989 by Luís Miquilena, Douglas Bravo and others in the aftermath of the *Caracazo*. Long an advocate of an alliance between soldiers and civilians, Quijada was a veteran of the attempted military coups of 1962.

In September, Quijada's commission revealed that at least half the country's 1,200 judges were guilty of corruption or incompetence, and should be sacked. Checking through the files of the National Judges Council, the organization responsible for investigating complaints against the judiciary, the commission had discovered that 4,000 complaints had been made in the past ten years against judges and prosecutors.

The corruption and incompetence of the judicial system has been known about for years, and many of the complaints against it concerned the failure to mount trials of corrupt politicians and bankers. One member of Quijada's commission, Carlos Tablante, denounced 'the judicial power in Venezuela' as 'a refuge of illegality, vagrancy and corruption', and he recalled that corrupt judges had dropped charges against two dozen bankers accused of the banking scandal in 1994 that had 'nearly bankrupted the financial system'. In spite of a public outcry, the charges against the bankers had been dropped

Yet what now made the situation more serious and explosive was the fact that most of the prison population – some 23,000 people – had never been brought to trial. President Chávez had issued a new penal code by decree on 1 July, as he was entitled to do while waiting for the exact wording of the new constitution. His decree was designed to modernize the judicial system and to give suspects the presumption of innocence and the guarantee of a swift trial. Its publication inevitably encouraged prisoners to think that something might soon be done.

At the end of September, riots broke out at a number of different prisons throughout the country, and a dozen prisoners were killed. At one prison outside Caracas, the National Guard was sent in with two tanks to restore order. The appalling state, even by the standards of Latin America, of the prisons of Venezuela had been well known for years, and the dreadful conditions had frequently sparked off large-scale riots. More than 500 prisoners were killed in 1998. Yet President Chávez was pledged to make things better. Judicial reform had been high on his list of priorities, now prison reform would have to be tackled as well.

In the first week of October, the Constituent Assembly declared a 'prisons emergency' that proved to be an impressive example of government on the hoof. In his Sunday morning radio programme on 3 October 1999, Chávez announced that teams of judges and prosecutors, together with human rights activists and priests, had gone into four of the country's most dangerous prisons to try to speed up prosecution and sentencing. He said that the government wanted to accelerate justice for prisoners awaiting trial, and to speed up the implementation of the new penal code. He thought that many people could be released immediately because of the length of time they had already served, while the prison teams hoped to clear 6,000 cases of prisoners awaiting trial by the end of the year. A day-release scheme was promoted to enable prisoners to work outside the prison during the day.

Chávez also hoped that the prisons would be able to begin to segregate prisoners awaiting trial according to the crimes they were accused of committing. In many prisons, people accused of being pickpockets shared cells with murder suspects. He told his radio audience that the National Guard had spent the weekend sweeping the prisons for weapons, and said that prison guards often confiscated them and sold them back to the prisoners.

The crisis in the prisons refocused attention on the reform of the judiciary. Judges in Venezuela were traditionally appointed by the majority party in Congress. Even the members of the Supreme Court were chosen by the party in power. While a quarter of the Court held permanent positions, the rest lacked any independence and could be dismissed at will. They were at their most vulnerable if they took action against politicians or their business partners, or moved against the presidents of powerful commercial concerns. Corruption charges against President Jaime Lusinchi had been held up by the Supreme Court for years. The recommendations of an investigating magistrate that he should be put on trial were simply ignored. Although one member of the Supreme Court had resigned in protest in 1992, and a group of intellectuals had urged the rest of the Court to do the same, nothing ever happened, and the Lusinchi case faded away.

Quijada's commission drafting legal clauses for the new constitution suggested new procedures for the selection and training of judges, and ways of supervising their activity, similar to those of the United States. It was even suggested that candidates for the Supreme Court might have to face public hearings as well as background investigation. While some hostile critics thought that the reforms would take years to have an effect, most people agree that the advances made by the Chávez government in this area have all been beneficial.

18

ALI RODRÍGUEZ ARAQUE AND THE
NEW POLITICS OF OIL

The increase in the oil price has not been the result of a war or
the full moon. No. It is the result of an agreed strategy, a change
of 180 degrees in the policy of previous governments and of
Petróleos de Venezuela . . . Now the world knows that there is a
serious government in Venezuela . . .

President Chávez, May 1999

Venezuela's future depends on the way that the government of President Chávez reorganizes the exploitation and commercialization of oil,
the industry that has transformed the country over the past eighty
years. This reorganization is of more than national interest, since
Venezuela provides the bulk of US oil imports.

Much of the oil comes from Lake Maracaibo, a great expanse of
water caught between the Andes and the Caribbean that has become
one of the man-made wonders of the world. A strangely romantic
place, the lake is the legacy of the bold pioneering days of capitalism
when taming and exploiting nature was done with simple technologies
and with the ingenuity and brute strength of workers. Today, it is an
unmitigated ecological disaster.

The lake's tear-drop shape is familiar to anyone who has ever studied a map of South America. Filled with Christmas tree derricks, a forest of four-legged metal masts sticking up from the surface of the water, it evokes memories of early movies with an oil industry background, or the sepia photographs in old encyclopaedias.

The real thing far surpasses the folk memory, and there are surprises too. Lake Maracaibo is not a place for tourist pedaloes; beribbonned captains drive brass-gleaming launches with pride and skill across the grey waters of this vast inland sea. This is a serious work environment, swarming with skilled men who know what they are about: divers, engineers, experts in rig construction.

The oil installations, thousands of them, are all the same but different: a small platform on four legs, festooned with pipes, accessible only by ladder; a construction with arms that move up and down remorselessly, like a Van Gogh sluice-gate in the Camargue; a gigantic raft covered with metal masts lashed to six immense barrels: a concrete erection with taps and tanks, and a cornucopia of tube work. In the centre of the lake stands a great platform familiar from the North Sea, a giant among pygmies. Rooted on three legs, the oil it is pumping out comes from 20,000 feet below the surface.

The practice of extracting oil from beneath the waters of a lake has gone on for nearly a century, and is now rendered commonplace by the elephantine technology that can secure it from the bottom of the sea. What still makes Lake Maracaibo rather special is that its surface stands far above the level of the surrounding countryside. So much oil has been taken from the Maracaibo basin since the 1920s that the surrounding land is steadily sinking into the huge hole that is left behind. The fields around the lake drop down a little lower every year.

Disaster might have struck had this not been an area developed originally by Royal Dutch Shell. The Dutch know a thing or two about low-lying land, and they are familiar with the construction of dikes. Years ago, with considerable ingenuity, Dutch engineers built a wall around the lake, and allowed the houses and the installations on the landward side to gently subside behind this protecting stockade. The surrounding terrain is now some 5 metres below sea level, and it continues to collapse evenly at the rate of between 15 and 20 centimetres a year. It would probably descend further and faster if the engineers did not also pump in water to fill the oil-vacated spaces.

This sense that something is being permanently removed, the reality of physical diminishment, is one of the reasons why all Venezuelans have such a passionate attachment to their state oil company. For decades their national patrimony was siphoned off by the great American and European oil companies, principally Shell and Mobil and Exxon. Generations of nationalist historians and politicians perceived this as a scandal, and the belief that the nation was being robbed remains deeply implanted in the national psyche.

Two events, one in 1943, the other in 1976, are celebrated as great and historic moments when the country stood up to the oil companies. In 1943, the government of General Isaías Medina Angarita took advantage of wartime scarcity to oblige the companies to comply with Venezuelan tax laws and to limit their concessions to a period of 40 years. In 1976, after only 30 years, President Carlos Andrés Pérez secured the agreement of the 14 principal foreign companies to a negotiated withdrawal from the country. On 1 January, the state oil company, Petróleos de Venezuela SA (PdVSA), took over their assets, which included 11,000 oil wells, 11 oil refineries, and 14 oil tankers. The package also contained pipelines, port terminals and innumerable office buildings.

Initially, the three largest of the nationalized companies continued to maintain their individual status: Royal Dutch Shell became known as Maraven; Exxon's Creole Petroleum Company as Lagoven; and Mobil Oil as Llanoven. Maraven and Lagoven even kept their separate corporate identities, one very European and carefree, the other very American and authoritarian. Essentially they were still competitors. The complex of old Dutch buildings in Maraven's lakeside town of Lagunillas remained untouched, and in spite of the palm trees, it continued to look like an old-fashioned Dutch village, with verandahs and high-pitched roofs. At the humming heart of a centre of late twentieth-century technology, you half expect someone to come down the street in clogs.

Like oil companies elsewhere in the world, Venezuela's newly nationalized enterprises spent much time searching for fresh sources of oil. Once there was a panic that it would all disappear, yet soon it was popping up everywhere. At Lake Maracaibo, they simply began drilling deeper. The oil may be more difficult to extract, but there is plenty of it. Large reserves have been located further to the south, in the state of Barinas, on the slopes of the Andes.

Over the years, the state oil company has not been immune to the pressures of globalization and privatization. These began under the government of President Pérez in 1989, and were continued with the so-called 'Apertura' or 'Opening [to the private sector]' that was continued by the government of President Caldera. Foreign companies were allowed to engage in joint ventures with the state oil company, and Shell and BP proudly re-opened their service stations in the capital to show that they were in business again. Petróleos de Venezuela had produced a draft investment plan in 1991, for US$65 billion, which envisaged a third of the capital coming from the private sector.

In 1997, the entire management of Petróleos de Venezuela was reorganized, and the individual companies within it, like Maroven and Lagoven, the hangover from the previous era, were finally abolished. The state company was now divided up in another way, three new divisions being created, one for exploration and production, another for marketing and manufacturing, and a third for services. The management and employees of the company were only just beginning to adjust to these dramatic changes when the new government arrived in 1999. One of the first changes made was to set up a fourth division to oversee the gas industry.

The new man in charge, as minister of energy and mines, was Ali Rodríguez Araque, a 60-year-old former guerrilla commander who had been the oil expert of La Causa R and of Patria Para Todos. Born in Mérida in 1937, Rodríguez Araque studied law and economics at the Universidad Central in Caracas and the Universidad de los Andes in Mérida. He had fought in the hills of Falcón state in the 1960s with Douglas Bravo, but after the collapse of the guerrilla war, and a period in the Partido de la Revolución de Venezuela, he parted company with Bravo. He joined up with Alfredo Maneiro's La Causa R, and worked as a labour lawyer in Ciudad Guayana.

In 1983, he was elected to Congress, supported by La Causa R, from the state of Bolívar, and in November 1998 he was elected as a senator for Patria Para Todos. During the Caldera government, from 1994 to 1997, he had an influential position in Congress as the president of its 'committee on energy and mines'. He had been closely involved in the congressional overseeing of contracts during the opening up of the oil industry to foreign markets. When the PPT joined the Chávez electoral alliance, he became Chávez's chief adviser on oil matters.

The first task in government of Rodríguez Araque was to reassert the primacy of his ministry over the state oil company. Petróleos de Venezuela had been run for years as a corporatist enterprise, a state within the state, a vast conglomerate dispensing favours and bribes. With a rapid changeover of personnel, including the replacement of Chávez's first choice to run the company, Rodríguez Araque's initial objectives were achieved.

The second task was to radically alter Venezuela's policy towards Opec, the Organization of Petroleum Exporting Countries. Venezuela had had a low reputation within Opec during the 1990s, when the policy of 'Apertura' was in operation, being seen as a member state that ignored all the guidelines. Successive Venezuelan governments had tried to go it alone. They had all but abandoned Opec, disregarding the quotas set and trying to jack up production by bringing in foreign companies to develop new oil fields.

The Chávez government had a different and well-defined internationalist strategy from the start. Rodríguez Araque ordered a change of direction, insisting on investment cuts at Petróleos de Venezuela. He was determined to cooperate with Opec, and to work towards securing a stable oil price. He journeyed round the Opec countries, and also sought to secure the cooperation of Latin American oil producers. Mexico, which is not a member of Opec, and competes with Venezuela in the lucrative US market, was persuaded to curb its planned production increases.

Finally, after an Opec meeting in March 1999, Venezuela cut back its output by 4 per cent to 2.72 million barrels a day, and announced that it had plans to make further cutbacks both on production and on exploration. In May, celebrating his first 100 days in power, President Chávez proudly explained what had happened:

> The increase in the oil price has not been the result of a war or the full moon. No. It is the result of an agreed strategy, a change of 180 degrees in the policy of previous governments and of Petróleos de Venezuela. First, we decided to respect the cutbacks in production agreed with Opec and with Mexico. Secondly, we decided to increase the level of cutbacks. Now the world knows that there is a serious government in Venezuela, and a new leadership in PdVSA . . .

Later in the year, in September, a correspondent for the *Financial Times*, Robert Corzine, noted that the previous few months had proved to be 'one of the more successful periods in the history of Opec's attempts to control the oil price'. Not only had its member countries stuck by the production cuts, and avoided the previous practice of 'quota cheating', but non-Opec members, like Britain and Norway, had been unable to take up the slack.

By the end of the year, Venezuela thought that the oil price was now high enough. Rodríguez Araque argued that Opec should now agree on a broad band within which the price could be sustained by adding or cutting output. Chávez proposed that a meeting of Opec heads of state should be held in Caracas in the year 2000, and he sent out invitations to, among others, Saddam Hussein of Iraq, Muammar Gadafy of Libya and the president of Iran.

The other significant innovation introduced by the Chávez government has been the modification of the macro-economic sta-bilization fund set up by the previous government. The Fondo de

Estabilización Macroeconómica was a special fund designed to supplement the government's income in the event of a collapse in the international oil price. The idea was to even out the volatility in international prices. If the price of oil went above US$14 a barrel, the extra revenue was to be channelled into the fund. Rodríguez Araque decided to drop the benchmark to US$9 a barrel. This was a conservative figure, but not out of line with the low oil price of recent years. Venezuelan crude had sold at US$16.6 in 1997, and had dropped to US$10.75 in 1998.

In reality, the price went way above US$9 in the course of 1999, pouring large sums into the stabilization fund. From US$11.95 in March 1999, before the Opec meeting, it had risen above US$20 later in the year.

The new relationship with Opec and the increase in the oil price, which was generally accepted with a good grace by the outside world, was one of the major success stories of Chávez's first year in government. But it left pending the conflictive question of the future of the state oil company.

Many influential citizens outside the government argued forcibly that individuals should have the right to a slice of the country's oil wealth. Alberto Quirós, once the head of Maraven, argued in newspaper articles that Venezuelan citizens should have the right to buy shares in their national oil company. Under the clauses of the new constitution, this would not be allowed to happen. The state would continue to keep a tight rein on the company.

Quirós argued in favour of allowing the company to sell 10 per cent of its stock so that the real worth of the company could be ascertained. He also thought that the company's financial resources, if suitably distributed, could help provide the basis for private pension funds.

For nationalists within the armed forces and within the Chávez government, these were dangerous proposals. Yet Rodríguez Araque himself was not without some revolutionary ideas. Interviewed in May 1998 by Maria Cristina Iglesias, when still in charge of the oil policy of Patria Para Todos in Congress, he gave an outline of a strategy that would involve individual Venezuelan investors buying shares in the state oil company:

> The idea was that during the period of exploration, which involves some risk, investment would only come from Petróleos de Venezuela and from international capital. Once suitable oil fields had been identified, some adjustments would be made: international capital would be allowed a maximum participation of 49 per cent, and Petróleos de Venezuela would also have a percentage share.
>
> The way would then be open for Venezuelan savers and investors to purchase share capital in the companies and consortia that would be set up to produce the oil. None of this, of course, would subtract from the legitimate remuneration due to foreign investors, who had taken the risks during the period of exploration. Such a programme would, without doubt, have attracted the solid backing of international capital.

In 1999, none of this had yet happened, but everyone could see that the writing was on the wall.

19

THE ECONOMIC PROGRAMME OF
THE CHÁVEZ GOVERNMENT

Our project is neither statist nor neo-liberal; we are exploring the middle ground, where the invisible hand of the market joins up with the visible hand of the state: as much state as necessary, and as much market as possible.

President Chávez, 2 February 1999

Venezuela may enjoy huge oil revenues but these are rapidly mopped up by a tiny percentage of the population. The great majority of the country is permanently poor and hungry. While the top 10 per cent of the population of 23 million receives half the national income, 40 per cent, according to an estimate of 1995, lives in 'critical poverty'. An estimated 80 per cent, according to the figures for 1996, earns the minimum wage or less. As if this was not enough, the situation has been growing dramatically worse. Real purchasing power declined by 35 per cent between 1989 and 1995.

These statistics are well known to President Chávez and his government, and he constantly tells foreign visitors how difficult it is to explain how such a rich country can at the same time be so desperately poor. He is also aware that he can wave no magic wand. Much of his time is spent, with Christian rhetoric, in urging the poor to be patient and the rich to acquire some sense of solidarity with the people with whom they are obliged to share the country.

Yet although disguised and not fully formulated, the outline of an economic policy can be discerned. In spite of all his rhetoric against neo-liberalism, Chávez is desperate for foreign investment. He has to steer a difficult and almost impossible course, telling his nationalist country what it wants to hear, and making the right kind of reassuring noises that will not frighten the foreign investors. In this, of course, he has the warm support of Fidel Castro. According to Fausto Masa, a usually well-informed journalist, Castro told Chávez that 'his principal preoccupation was to secure the last US dollar for Cuba, because the only revolutionary way to secure development today is to open up the entire country to foreign investors'.

What is good enough for revolutionary Cuba is fine for Venezuela, and Chávez has followed this implicit instruction. The US ambassador in Caracas, John Maisto, spent much of 1999 trying to get the Chávez government to sign the treaty on the promotion and protection of foreign investment that all other Latin American governments have been obliged to sign. Maisto tried to get the treaty signed before the first meeting of the Constituent Assembly, knowing full well that the nationalist Assembly would be adverse to its terms. He turned out to be knocking at an open door. Chávez's cabinet quietly agreed to sign, in October, and Chávez ensured that this was done when he was out of the country. 'He now goes round making speeches guaranteeing stability and investment,' one disillusioned leftist economist told me.

Yet during his first year in office, his radical supporters made no objection to this strategy. Many of them were involved with another project, debating in the Constituent Assembly the parameters of a future economic policy rather than contemplating the here-and-now. A strong element in their programme, in any case, has been the encouragement of local investors. This was always part of the economic policy of La Causa R and of Patria Para Todos, an attempt to befriend the small independent businessman and the entrepreneur against the large state barons and their commercial and banking friends.

Economic opinion abroad was divided in its initial attitude to the Chávez phenomenon. 'You're looking at a very, very ugly recession next year if oil prices don't recover,' said a pessimistic spokesman for Merrill Lynch in New York a week or two after the election in December 1998. He added gloomily that Chávez would 'have to be Superman to pull the economy out of trouble'. Other outsiders were equally glum at that time. 'We just think the risks are too high at the moment,' said an analyst at Deutsche Bank in New York.

The pessimism turned out to be ill-founded. Oil prices did recover. Yet investors inside Venezuela had always been less alarmed. Most of them realized that things would certainly have been worse if Chávez had failed to win. The Caracas stock market went up after the election as these local investors, having moved out during the election in case of a freak result, came flooding back. 'When you see the flows,' said the man from Merrill Lynch cheerfully, 'it was really the locals bringing their money back.'

In spite of all the rhetoric, President Chávez in office has turned out to be a pragmatic ruler. He believes, essentially, that the combination of honest men and women and honest government will provide good government. He is passionately hostile to 'corruption', of which there was no shortage in the past, and fiercely against the philosophy of 'savage neo-liberalism' imposed on the world by the United States. Yet he often finds it difficult to describe just what it is that he intends to put in its place. His first speech as president on 2 February 1999, gave few details about what lay ahead:

> Our project is neither statist nor neo-liberal; we are exploring the middle ground, where the invisible hand of the market joins up with the visible hand of the state: as much state as necessary, and as much market as possible.

The sound-bite is admirable, but as directions for a minister in charge of the economy, it could only be read in one way: keep to the existing course.

'He's very radical everywhere else,' one academic economist told me, 'but he's conservative in the economic sphere. He's very positive and firm on foreign policy, but there is nothing remotely similar in the economic sphere. He concentrates his attacks on corrupt politicians, but he never mentions the bankers, and they were just as bad.'

Yet while Chávez personally has no great interest in economics, his political supporters in the MAS and in Patria Para Todos have certainly evolved something approaching an economic programme over the years, though it might be more accurate to describe it as an attitude. During the course of 1999, the economic decisions and actions of the government received little publicity, but the economic debate in the Constituent Assembly secured many headlines. Chávez supporters in the Assembly, both leftist civilians and retired military officers, were determined that the state should continue to play a significant role in the economy. This was the majority view in the Assembly, and certainly in the country as well.

Yet this controlling group had very disparate ambitions. Many from the MAS still hankered for the days when the state had an active developmental role; those from the Patria Para Todos, reflecting the greener values of La Causa R, longed for a smaller state with fewer opportunities for corruption, and expressed their concern about the future of small enterprises and about pollution and the environment.

Despite these differences, almost everyone in the Assembly was united in their desire to see off the neo-liberal fundamentalists, whose nostrums played no part in the final formulation of the new constitution. Yet the victory was more apparent than real. While only a handful were prepared to see Petróleos de Venezuela sold off to private interests, almost everyone agreed that it would be reasonable to make deals with foreign oil companies. In practice, it appeared that significant parts of the economic policy developed during the 1990s – which had opened up the oil industry to foreign participation and begun a process of privatization – would be continued.

This appearance of continuity was reinforced by the presence in the cabinet of Maritza Izaguirre, who had been inherited from the

Caldera administration, as the economics minister. She resigned in June 1999 to be replaced by her deputy José Rojas, who had also worked there under Caldera. 'Poor Maritza really didn't know what was happening,' I was told, 'and José Rojas is now finding the same, although he's a supporter of the Quinta República.'

The change making the ministers nervous was the introduction of military personnel into the senior reaches of the public administration. 'The military are everywhere,' one senior economic adviser explained to me. 'It sometimes seems as though there is a secret project that you don't quite know about. There really is a military party. In some of the ministries, it's a case of dual power.' Senior military officers have in fact now been placed in all the principal ministries, including Petróleos de Venezuela. 'Many come from the lower classes,' my academic economist told me, 'and will tell you "my dad was a worker". Yet they have studied at the university, and their intellectual preparation is pretty good; when I was teaching at the university there were three officers out of a class of twenty. But their mentality is rather different, and they are certainly autocratic. Some are on the left, but I have met some *Pinochetista* officers.'

Most of the officers introduced into government are at a level just below the top. They are watching and waiting, and keeping their eyes open. But one central figure is running his own show, and he certainly isn't a *Pinochetista*. Colonel William Fariñas is the president of the Fondo Unico Social (FUS), or the Social Fund, a new and potentially powerful creation that links together a number of earlier government organizations that used to deal with health and social welfare.

The Fondo Unico, together with the Banco del Pueblo, or People's Bank, is one of a raft of new organizations designed to carry through the social policies that are aimed at improving the health and welfare of the poor majority of the population. The political impact of such institutions echo down the years: Eva Perón used to run the ministry of social welfare in Argentina in the 1940s, and it served as her power base when trying to improve the conditions of the poor. The Velasco government in Peru in the 1970s had a somewhat similar institution set up by the military, the Sistema Nacional de Apoyo a la Movilización Social (Sinamos), the National System to Support Social Mobilization. Sinamos sounded brilliant on paper, but was a disastrous failure in practice.

Colonel Fariñas, like other senior officers in the Chávez government, has done time at the university. He was a professor of strategic planning and social policy at the Universidad Central in Caracas. He also has a doctorate in organizational training. As a retired air force colonel, he has many heroes: Bolívar, of course; the Sacred Heart of Jesus, the Virgin Mary Auxiliadora; the Archangel Michael; – and Che Guevara.

> Che is the one single figure who represents commitment and altruism, and complete dedication to the cause of the people – everywhere in the world. He is an icon for all revolutionaries, as he is for me . . . he has been always, ever since I was a student and began to hold revolutionary convictions. The revolutionary spirit that animates the military and other citizens taking part in this process has been nourished on the thoughts and ideals of Che, and of what once were the events of May in France . . .

This sixties' revolutionary is in charge of an organization with huge political potential and a large budget. The budget derives partly from the ordinary budget of the earlier organizations that it has gobbled up, and partly from the Fondo de Estabilización Macroeconómica (FEM) that channels oil money to government projects. Indeed the FUS will receive 40 per cent of the FEM's budget.

The Fondo will help to fund schools and hospitals, and even churches, but its most ambitious new funding project is the 'Bolívar Plan 2000', one of Chávez's most original ideas. The details were announced on 27 February 1999, within weeks of his inauguration. The idea is to mobilize the spare capacity of the armed forces, to link up with local community groups, and to make an impact on Venezuela's increasingly derelict social infrastructure. Soldiers will make available to local communities their barracks, their sports grounds, and their canteens. They will go out into the community and help rebuild roads and schools.

The 'Bolivar Plan' was designed to be implemented in three stages. Stage one, called Pro-País, would involve the armed forces in the provision of social services. Stage two, Pro-Pátria, would involve the military in helping local communities to seek local solutions to their problems; and Stage three, Pro-Nación, would launch the country on the road towards economic self-sufficiency and sustainable development.

In the Pro-País phase, the country was divided into 25 action zones, and some 40,000 soldiers and volunteers began work on the reconstruction of roads, health centres and schools, working with the local authorities. President Chávez told reporters that 'mobile field hospitals' would be dispatched to remote villages and slums 'as if to a war zone'. In December, after the terrible mudslides in the coastal state of Vargas, the war zone metaphor proved uncomfortably apt.

20

A NEW AGRICULTURAL FUTURE
FOR VENEZUELA

If rice were the national dish, 'we would change the mentality of the Venezuelans, who would eat mangos instead of apples, arepas instead of hamburgers, and rice instead of pasta'.

Federico Cappellin, *El Universal*, 2 November 1999

I travelled to the sandy shores of the Orinoco by stretch limo. It had not been my intention to do anything of the kind. The car was parked outside the the Caracas bus station, perceived as a dangerous part of town where you need to keep your wits about you – and to clutch your wallet firmly – and I couldn't resist it.

My initial destination was Cabruta, a forgotten village at the junction of the country's two great rivers, the Orinoco and the Apure, but buses only make the journey at night. The *llanos*, Venezuela's vast plains that provide grass for cattle in their millions, become unbearably hot during the day, so drivers familiar with the road sensibly schedule their journeys when it's cooler. But I had no desire to sleep in a bus for eight hours; I wanted to see the great plains.

An offer by Gabriel, an overweight and jovial driver with the long black hair of the indigenous people, seemed the answer. The proud owner of a limo stretched along the side of the pavement, he said he would take me on the long drive to the Orinoco for 50 dollars. There was only one small snag: he had never been there before, and perhaps if he had known more about the nature of the road he might have had second thoughts.

The stretch limo was an old Ford in various shades of off-white, much dented and severely scratched, but undoubtedly serviceable, and an object of uncommon interest in the Venezuelan countryside. Soldiers manning the small police posts along the road would stop us to embark on a short perfunctory search – and then to have a long discussion about the finer points of engine tuning. Gabriel is an enthusiastic Chávez supporter, and plays the tapes of the folksingers such as Ali Primera and Cristóbal Jiménez who extol the virtues of the president.

Soon there is something rather more basic to attend to. Every road trip in Latin America at some stage contains an involuntary stop to mend a puncture. Bus, lorry, van, car – all drivers use their tyres to the bitter end. Only when they are paper thin and go bang do their owners decide that a replacement is necessary. The bang came on a narrow busy stretch of road, and Gabriel carefully reversed the wounded limo onto a piece of hard ground. It is midday, over 100°F, and without a trace of shade, and Gabriel must weigh at least twenty stone, yet he leaps around with the alacrity of a younger, thinner, man, and within twenty minutes we are back on the road again.

More of a problem now is the condition of the road. This is a metalled highway, built in the days when Venezuela had more money than sense, with huge oil royalties and a government with a passion for infrastructure. But the original smooth surface has disappeared long since, and there is no money to mend it. The cost of travel now falls instead on the individual driver, obliged to pay for the repair to his shattered vehicle, shaken and shocked by the bumps. For Gabriel and his stretch limo, the problems are more dramatic. The front wheels may miss the potholes, but not the ones at the back. When that happens, the entire chassis scrapes along the ground. Miraculously, we survive.

Eight hours later, with ten minutes to spare before a violent orange sun disappeared beneath the rippled surface of the swiftly flowing Orinoco river, we drove majestically into the bedraggled settlement of Cabruta, admired by one and all.

Cabruta was established at the junction of the Orinoco and the Apure by the Jesuits, one of half a dozen mission stations constructed in this region in the early eighteenth century. When Alexander von Humboldt, the German scientist and traveller, came exploring here in 1800, the Jesuit missionaries had long gone, but the remains of the old settlements could still be seen, a handful of Indian families surviving by the shores of the Orinoco at Cabruta, La Encaramada, Urbana, Canichana, San Borja and El Raudal.

Cabruta today is now the fulcrum of 'the Apure–Orinoco axis', one of President Chávez's projects to develop and settle the centre-south of Venezuela. Above Cabruta stands a large rocky headland, and from there you can see the Orinoco stretching southwards towards Brazil and eastwards to the Atlantic. The Apure, which joins the Orinoco at this strategic spot, comes down from Colombia and the Andes far to the west. In these now empty lands President Chávez is hoping to develop agriculture in such a way that people currently living in the shanty towns of the great cities will be persuaded to move out into the countryside. He wants to create new economic centres in the sparsely populated east and south of the country in order to welcome migrants from the crowded cities of northern Venezuela.

This is under-inhabited cattle land, but it could also be used for the industrial production of rice and palm, two products where Chávez believes the country has a strong competitive advantage.

'Look, here is the Apure–Orinoco axis', he exclaimed when we were poring over the map together at his residence at La Casona in January 2000. His excitement was infectious. 'The land has been virtually abandoned; we won't have to build new towns here, we will simply strengthen the settlements that already exist.'

Chávez was also interested in another area, in the far west of the country, just to the north of the Apure–Orinoco axis. Here there would be a north–south axis, from Guasdualito close to the Colombian border to Lake Maracaibo. Chávez was showing me the settlement of La Fría on the map, an existing though abandoned farm project where the homeless survivors of the December floods might be resettled. Lying under the slopes of the Andes, close to the Colombian border, it was to be another pilot scheme for the ambitious long-term projects that he had in mind.

'It's a place in the state of Táchira, to the north of the Apure–Orinoco axis, to the north of San Cristóbal. Here is the village, with about 10,000 inhabitants. It's a wonderfully rich region, at the foot of the mountains, just to the south of Lake Maracaibo. I once worked there in a military unit, and we used to go out on patrol.'

He pulls forward the map again. 'Look, here is the frontier with Colombia, here is the international airport, here is an abandoned industrial site. Here is the land, here are some houses, and here we will put in a school, a workshop, and a road.'

All this had been built ten years ago in the days of Carlos Andrés Pérez. 'They spent thousands and thousands of *bolívares*, and then Pérez himself abandoned it. They began to build a motorway to San Cristóbal, the capital, but it came to a stop because they never made the tunnels through the mountains. The road is still there, but without the tunnels.'

Chávez told me he had scheduled a visit to La Fría for the following week. 'Why don't you come with us?' he said abruptly, and I explained apologetically that I had a return ticket to London in three days' time. 'Well, we could go the day after tomorrow, on Wednesday. We were planning to go somewhere else then, to Zulia, but that can easily wait.'

He summoned up his aide-de-camp, sitting in view but out of earshot. 'Get me General Cruz Weffer on the phone,' he said, and within half a minute he was through to the chief of the general staff. 'Look, I think we'll go to La Fría on Wednesday. How much is ready? How many families have you got? What sort of state is it in?' He paused to listen to a stuttering reply. 'Well, tell them to get a move on. We'll come anyway; it doesn't matter if it's not all finished.'

I was being given a private introduction to that characteristic of

President Chávez which his close collaborators often find alarming: his military attention to detail and his capacity to make rapid decisions and to demand instant action. For most of the things he wants done, today is already too late.

So, early on Wednesday morning, with the sun barely over the hills that surround the city, I waited for him in the officers' lounge at the small airport of La Carlota in the centre of Caracas, where the Venezuelan air force is based, while a secret service agent spent time crawling under the sofas to check for bombs. When Chávez arrived, wearing his casual camouflage uniform and his red beret, we set off in the presidential plane and headed for the Colombian border, an hour's flight away. Half the cabinet came too.

We landed at the deserted airport, the grass growing between the squares of the concrete runway. A military band greets the president, and, after the usual military formalities, we climb into four large heli-copters to fly to a military farm nearby, at Guarumito. From the air, the settlement looks pitifully isolated, a huddle of tin roofs surrounded by the savannah stretching away into the distance. The indistinguish-ably similar territory of Colombia lies a couple of miles away.

On the ground, things look marginally more encouraging. We land on a piece of hard track beside a swamp where a small group of workers is busy repairing a dozen of the tin-roofed bungalows we had seen from the air. Most of them are wearing yellow rubber boots, but an officer is criticizing three boys who are wearing flip-flops. They say that their boots are wet. This is a military camp, and the military are providing the land and the houses for resettling the flood victims, but the officer is obviously keen that his workers should make a good impression on the president.

From the moment Chávez alights from his helicopter he is mobbed by a crowd that appears from nowhere. He makes his way slowly through to a large converted caravan that serves as a mobile training workshop. This is the civilian component in this military–civilian operation, run by the government's national training institute. It contains carpentry benches and simple electric saws. Chávez interrogates the education supervisor, a nervous civilian, and fires off a stream of questions. How long have you been here? When will it all begin? When are the teachers coming?

'The teachers are being selected,' says the supervisor apologetically, 'but none have arrived yet.'

'Yes,' says Chávez, 'we know all about that. People get involved, and then they leave. A month later and everything's back to square one. You have to be really careful how you choose.'

He continues to badger the wretched superviser. 'You've got to be more productive. Why don't you put up some tents, build another building, bring more people in.' He discovers that the superviser is spending time driving backwards and forwards every day from the town – only five minutes in the helicopter, an hour each way by car. 'You can't do that all the time,' he says, 'you'll get exhausted. Why don't you try staying here in a tent. Don't forget how important this job is. We are not teaching them so that they can go off somewhere else. We want people to stay here. We are colonizing the country with our own people. How many times have we failed in the past? We can't fail this time.'

The supervisor, in the tidy dark suit of a state official, nods in agreement, but he looks appalled.

While waiting for Chávez, who is caught by another crowd, I talk to Jorge Giordani, the minister of planning. Grey-haired, looking older than his years, he is the man behind the plan for internal development. A radical economist and a university professor, who studied at the Institute for Development Studies at the University of Sussex in the days of the late Dudley Seers, he had been the economic guru of the Movement to Socialism. Giordani had been working with his students on the formulation of a programme to revitalize the rural areas, and he tells me how he used to visit Chávez in prison. The two men got on well together, and he became Chávez's economics tutor, supervising his university thesis. As planning minister, he has brought in a team of university radicals to flesh out the president's plans. His ministry, Cordiplan, is responsible for the details of the proposed revolution in agriculture.

We move to an assembly room in the barracks where Chávez is

now interrogating the commanding officer. He discovers that some of the land here has been taken over by squatters who have been cutting down the trees and selling the wood. 'I want to know urgently who sold off the land. Anyone caught cutting down trees will go to prison. It's absolutely illegal. I want to know who owns the land round here in a 50 kilometre radius. I know there are lots of people who own land here who actually live in Miami or in London. We shall expropriate it. The new constitution allows us to do so, but we shall pay for it of course.'

Then he starts asking about what the land could produce. 'What used to be grown in this region? What did the Indians grow? Is milk production really the best idea, or would vegetables be better?' The audience start chipping in with their views, and eventually everyone agrees that this is good land for cattle. Chávez says sternly that he will soon return to see how they are getting on, and he warns them that he may fly in without warning.

We walk round to the bungalows that have already been refurbished and are about to be officially handed over to their new owners. They have been built in a circle, around a central plaza, and each has a patch of land out behind. Some makeshift awnings have been erected, but Chávez stands out in the centre in the burning midday sun for more than an hour. Most of the 24 families being provided with a house come from the sites of the coastal tragedy in December, some from Naiguata, though a handful come from a similar disaster nearby. One of these local men tells me that his maize and yucca plantation was carried away by the floods. 'We have no money, no capital, we need help,' he says. When I ask him to put his name in my notebook, he apologizes for not being able to write.

The families come up in turn, and Chávez talks to each of them. Usually it is a young man and a young woman, with two or three small children, though sometimes there is an older, more careworn couple. They walk up in their family group and he hands them their title deed, asks them about their experiences and their skills, and offers words of warning and advice. They go away with smiles on their faces. The houses are not gifts to the settlers, for they will live in them rent-free for only a year. After that, they will have to pay a regular quota to the cooperative that formally owns them.

When the formalities are finished, Chávez makes a short speech, saying that he has been warned by his chief of staff that his trip is already running three hours behind schedule. 'Never mind, we are going to do these things properly.' He knows it is important to provide some encouragement and some sense of ceremony as they take over their new homes.

'You are very daring to have come here,' he tells them, 'and to found a new town. It is not easy for anyone to move from the sea coast to the inland savannah. Yet just think, we only started two weeks ago, and in a few months' time there will be a thousand homes here.'

Guarumito, he reminds them, is the name of the indigenous people who used to live here. 'I know this region, these are some of the best lands in Venezuela. I've been here on several occasions to patrol the frontier.' He tells them not to be worried about the isolation. 'We are going to build a railway line that will pass near here, from the Apure river to Lake Maracaibo.'

He adds a final note of warning. 'Please don't call your roads or houses after me. I don't want to be remembered with anything like the "Raúl Leoni motorway"', and he recalls the extravagance of a previous president.

This has been a heart-warming occasion, the new settlers standing up proudly, the children waving the blue and yellow flag of Venezuela, and everyone close to tears. Chávez plays his role as the avuncular comforter, talking, asking questions, seeking answers and spreading a sense of optimism and goodwill.

Our gaggle of ministers and hangers-on moves back to the helicopters, and we fly off to view another abandoned project of the *ancien régime*, an immense and abandoned industrial park, said to be the largest in South America. Chávez again plunges into the waiting crowd, to discover what it is they want. They have been living here for some years, and they only want one thing: work. Then we clamber into a bus and drive slowly round the abandoned site.

Chávez conducts an impromptu seminar with his ministers, as the man in charge explains what used to happen in each empty shed and warehouse. They discuss what will be taken over, and how investors might be encouraged to move here if given sufficient tax breaks. The state can provide education and medical care, but there will be no repeat of the failed state enterprises of the 1970s. The private investor will have to be encouraged to set up the large and small projects necessary to revive the failures of the earlier era. The minister of industry tells me that if the military would assist with clearing up the site, it would be possible to establish 50 small enterprises, employing perhaps 20 people each, within the first year. Chávez wants everything to be done more quickly.

When we get back to the military base at La Fría, many hours late for lunch, Chávez holds an hour-long cabinet meeting to discuss what everyone has learnt, and what steps they should take next. We climb back into the presidential jet, and the meeting continues, and it was still going on at the airport terminal of La Carlota when I left to go home. Chávez stays on talking, with no signs of exhaustion, and returned to La Casona for more meetings later that night; his civilian ministers looked completely worn out, as indeed was I.

The resettlement of flood victims at La Fría is just one in a long line of experiments made by Latin American governments over the years to try to reverse the rural migration that has been asphyxiating the cities. There have been more failures than successes. In the early 1970s the radical military government in Peru permitted legalized squatting in the *pueblos jóvenes* (new settlements) established around Lima, but the strategy merely brought fresh immigration from the rural Andes to the coastal city, and made the shanty towns even larger.

Chávez wants to be more original than that, by transferring the surplus urban population to new agro-industrial developments far from the delights of the city. This is not the strategy of Pol Pot in Cambodia, for there is no suggestion of coercion. The scale is small and the time-scale long. Chávez told me that he was thinking of at least twenty years. Just conceivably, he might persuade a few thousand pioneers to take up the challenge, but it seems more likely that his projects will slow down the rate of rural–urban migration rather than reverse it. That in itself would be well worth the effort.

No president since the days of General Pérez Jiménez in the early 1950s has done much for agriculture in Venezuela. Chávez would like to make the country capable of feeding itself. At present, Venezuela imports more than half its food needs, 64 per cent in 1998. Where previous governments have concentrated on oil, or on industrial development, or on trade and commerce, the Chávez government will concentrate on agriculture. Vast areas of Venezuela lie fallow or unused. Cattle roam over innumerable acres that could be more productively used.

More than fifty years ago, people talked of 'sowing the oil', using the oil rent to improve agriculture. This never happened, and Chávez now plans that it will. In 1999, a small start was made with US$15 million allocated to peasant families to assist in the creation of new farming settlements in rural areas. The scheme was designed to increase production of such staples as rice and maize, milk and sugar, and cooking oil.

You might think that rice would be the staple diet of Venezuela, a hot country with great rivers and swamps. Yet nowadays the Venezuelans eat more wheat than rice, since imported wheat from the United States, at subsidized prices, is cheaper than home-grown rice. According to Federico Cappellín, a columnist in *El Nacional*, Venezuelans only eat 12 kilograms of rice per person per year, while in Colombia they eat 30 kilograms, in Brazil 48 kilograms, in Ecuador 58 kilograms, and in Peru 32 kilograms. Venezuelans make up for their failure to eat rice by consuming 65 kilograms a year of wheat imported from the United States.

Rice is grown in Venezuela, indeed more is produced at present than is locally consumed. Wheat of course is not a suitable crop for a tropical country. So to change the country's priorities, Chávez will have to change the national diet, promoting rice and maize instead of wheat-based pasta. Cappellín suggests that rice should be made the national dish, and that the new constitution should have declared it to be the 'national cereal'. In doing so, he wrote hopefully, 'we would change the mentality of the Venezuelans, who would eat mangos instead of apples, [maize] *arepas* instead of hamburgers, and rice instead of pasta'.

In one of the great shopping malls of Caracas, I made a list of the various places you could stop to eat. First there was 'Wendy's Old-Fashioned Hamburgers', illustrated with a North American girl with short curls and two ribbons. Next came the 'American Deli', with the Statue of Liberty included on its logo. Then the 'Italian Coffee Company', with street signs for Canal Street and Manhattan. These were followed by 'Good Time Ice Cream', 'Happy Time Ice Cream', 'Chip-a-Cookie', 'Dunkin' Donuts', the 'St Möritz chocolatier', and of course McDonalds. It is difficult to imagine that the cheerful young people who inhabit the shopping mall, with their North Americanized life-style, will want to eat *arepas* rather than hamburgers, or to exchange pasta for rice, yet this is the revolutionary change being required of them by the Chávez government as it seeks to reconstruct the country on more nationalist lines.

21

JOSÉ VICENTE RANGEL AND
THE CONDUCT OF FOREIGN AFFAIRS

Soviet power has collapsed, but that does not mean that neo-liberal capitalism has to be the model followed by the peoples of the West. If only for that reason, we invite China to keep its flag flying, because this world cannot be run by a universal police force that seeks to control everything.

President Chávez in Beijing, October 1999

President Chávez set out with high ambitions in the field of foreign policy. His aim was nothing less than the Bolivarian dream of the union of the peoples of Latin America. Others have paid lip service to this notion during the past half century, most notably Fidel Castro and Che Guevara. Castro, in his early days in power in Cuba, invoked the tradition of 'Our America', in the 'First Declaration of Havana' in 1960. With his wonderful sense of history, he eulogized 'the America that Bolívar, Hidalgo, Juárez, San Martín, O'Higgins, Sucre and Martí wished to see free'.

Che Guevara, in his guerrilla camp in Bolivia at Nancahuazú in December 1966, invoked the spirit of the continental revolution, drinking a toast to the new 'grito de Murillo' that his guerrilla group was making, echoing the cry of the lawyer in La Paz in

1809 that had been designed to spark off the liberation of Latin America.

The fascination of Hugo Chávez with the story of Bolívar and the Bolivarian project of emancipation continues this tradition of radical American leadership, and, as a Venezuelan, he can draw on his own country's rather special relationship with the Liberator. In an interview with Agustín Blanco Muñoz in 1995, he argued that 'the geopolitical concept of Bolívar, envisaging the union of the continent, still has tremendous contemporary force'.

> None of his generals at the time of independence, at least none of his Venezuelan generals, had this vision, this notion of uniting all these balkanized territories of Latin America in order to confront the imperial power of the north. Now everyone is searching and struggling towards this goal, not just the Venezuelans but all of Latin America.

An emphasis on Latin American economic integration is, of course, nothing new; this has been the established rhetoric of almost all governments for several decades. The emphasis that President Chávez had placed on politics is by contrast fresh and interesting. He aims to follow in the steps of Bolívar, and to convene a *congreso anfictiónico* in Caracas in the year 2000 of all the Bolivarian states of the continent, just as Bolívar did in Panama in 1826.

> The twentieth century was a lost century. Our peoples lived better in the previous century than in this one, much better. So this can only be the union envisaged by Bolívar. *La patria* for all of us is America; and union is fundamental. Everyone has shared this aim: Martí, O'Higgins and Artígas – and Sandino and Perón said so too. The union of all our peoples.

His strategy, he says, 'is directed towards the creation of an alliance, a great Latin American and Caribbean union'. What he wants is 'a community of nations and states'.

This, he implies, must be politically driven, but he does not forget the economics. 'We have defined as a priority in the definition of our foreign policy the integration of the three entities that surround Venezuela' – the Caribbean (the Cuenca del Caribe), the Amazon (Mercosur and Brazil), and the Andes (the Comunidad Andino).

Chávez explained to Heinz Dieterich, an Argentine journalist, in May 1999, that he hoped Venezuela would soon be able to 'press the accelerator' on the integration of the Andean Community, Mercosur and the Cuenca del Caribe, 'including of course Central America up to Mexico, Cuba, and Santo Domino, and all the islands of the Caribbean'.

'Why,' he asks rhetorically, 'don't we think in terms of a currency, not the dollar, but a Latin American currency, just like the euro of the European Community . . .'

Chávez has extended this idea of integration to the military field. At the beginning of November 1999, he addressed a party of time-servers from the Andean parliament, a harmless talking-shop whose members are chosen from the national parliaments of the Andean republics. Chávez woke them from their slumbers to suggest that they should consider developing a Latin American Nato, a project for a continental military alliance which could hardly have been further from their minds.

Nato, of course, is an institution organized by the United States, which operates largely for its benefit. Chávez, by a sleight of hand, was suggesting something rather different – a Latin American Nato without the United States. For many years, of course, a Latin American Nato of sorts has been in existence, called the Junta Interamericana de Defensa. Its headquarters is in Washington, and although some US generals like to speak in Spanish, its meetings are conducted in English. Several Latin American armies, in return for political support, receive extensive economic assistance from Washington, and almost all of them have a privileged entrance into the American second-hand arms market. Two countries in particular, Mexico and Argentina, have established close military relations with the United States that amount to a formal military alliance.

Yet not every Latin American officer has been happy about this arrangement. Many remember the Falklands/Malvinas war in 1992 when their United States ally sided with the British against Argentina. Others recall the military interventions of the United States in the past decade – in Panama and in Haiti (and in Grenada in the 1980s). Everyone recognizes that the threat of intervention in Colombia is high.

There is another military concern. The United States occupied Panama in 1989 and then abolished the Panamanian National Guard. Many officers in Venezuela fear, and Chávez has given voice to this fear, that this is now the American programme for the continent. Abolish the armed forces!

Foreign affairs in the Chávez government is in the competent and emollient hands of José Vicente Rangel, an experienced politician and a natural diplomat, and a man well known for his sentimental attachment to the Cuban Revolution and for his hostility towards the policies of the United States towards Latin America. Three times presidential candidate of the left, and for decades one of Venezuela's most outspoken journalists – with a weekly programme on radio and televison and a Sunday column in *El Universal* – Rangel is now, at the age of 70, charged with implementing Chávez's 'Bolivarian' foreign policy.

On the walls of his office, beside the statutory portrait of Bolívar, only one other picture hangs, a photograph of José Ignácio Arcaya, the foreign minister in the early 1960s who – uniquely – refused to endorse the United States' demand that the Latin American countries should boycott Fidel Castro's Cuba. Arcaya is remembered as the 'minister of dignity'. In a bleak decade he did the right thing. His son is Chávez's minister of the interior. Rangel's son is a Chávez supporter in the Constituent Assembly. The photograph is well chosen.

Broad-shouldered, white-haired and with a military moustache, José Vicente Rangel conjures up the image of a genial Colonel Blimp or, perhaps, of an insurance salesman, which of course he once was. Exiled to Spain in the 1950s during the dictatorship of General Pérez Jiménez, he took up the first job he was offered.

Born in 1929, in the days of the old dictator Juan Vicente Gómez, Rangel is a product of the radical euphoria of the era after 1945. Educated at the conservative Catholic Liceo La Salle in Barquisimento, he studied law at the university of Mérida, and then moved on to the Universidad Central in Caracas, ever a hotbed of radical politics. He had originally joined Jovito Villalba's Unión Republicano Democrático (URD), and was a member of the party's national leadership for many years, from 1950 to 1963.

Much of his political life has been influenced by his deep distrust of Acción Democrática, and particularly of its first leader, Rómulo Betancourt, who adopted a bitterly anti-communist and pro-United States position. This enduring hostility to Acción Democrática is shared by Chávez, and is one of the characteristics of all the senior figures in his government. Rangel finally left the URD in 1964, when Villalba allied himself with the hated party. In the 1970s, he moved towards the Movimiento al Socialismo that had split from the Communist Party; he was their presidential candidate on several occasions, without being an actual member.

So why had this once fiery leftist teamed up with Comandante Chávez? By happenstance, he told me, he had been aware of the existence of Chávez before the failed coup of February 1992 brought him to national attention. Rangel's son, José Vicente junior, had studied at the military academy in Caracas in the 1980s. His commanding officer (and indeed his tutor) had been Hugo Chávez. At weekends, the (rather famous) former presidential candidate of the left and the (wholly unknown) future coup leader would meet. Later, Rangel was to visit Chávez in Yare prison.

Paradoxically, Rangel junior was obliged to leave the academy. It was thought that this son of a well-known leftist must be trying to infiltrate the military for the purpose of promoting a coup. No one realised at the time that the commanding officer rather than the raw recruit was behind the plotting.

One of José Vicente Rangel's tasks as foreign minister has been to try to improve the image of the president abroad. Throughout the presidential campaign of 1998, the conservative opposition painted

Chávez in the most sombre hues: at best Nasser and Ataturk, at worst Hitler and Mussolini. John Maisto, the American ambassador in Caracas, refused to grant him a visa to visit the United States when he was a candidate, and greeted his election with considerable alarm. An unambitious career diplomat who did not intend to go down in history as the man who had 'lost' Venezuela, Maisto believed Chávez to be a dangerous and anti-democratic *golpista*. 'I don't know anyone in Venezuela who thinks that Chávez is a democrat,' he is alleged to have said. Richard Wilkinson, the British ambassador, and the other European ambassadors, took a more measured view. Chávez was invited to Britain in 1998 and made an excellent impression on everyone he met.

After his election as president in December 1998, Chávez set out on a round of visits to the countries of Latin America, notably to Mexico, Brazil and Argentina. He was politely received everywhere, although most of the other presidents clearly hoped that his Bolivarian dream of continental integration would remain just attractive rhetoric. He went to Rome to see the Pope and to Spain to see the king. He needed to shake off the negative image that had been constructed for him.

After some months as president, he repeated the exercise. In September 1999, he spoke at the United Nations in New York, and pressed the flesh in Washington. The Americans had remained hostile during the early months of the Chávez government, and in August 1999, after the arguments between the old Congress and the new Constituent Assembly had broken out into the streets of Caracas, Washington expressed its anxieties openly.

The situation in Venezuela is a matter of 'growing concern', said James Foley, a State Department spokesman, on 30 August, and he earnestly expressed hope that all parties would 'come to agreement about how to exercise power' and how 'to assure the establishment of a constitution that preserves Venezuela's long-standing commitment to democracy'.

Yet with Chávez actually present in Washington, the atmosphere began to change. He won over the editors of the *Washington Post* at a breakfast meeting. 'He spoke in colourful and dramatic images,' according to Nora Boustany's report, 'about the pain he felt from Venezuelans as he roamed the countryside on horseback and on foot after he finished a jail term five years ago for trying to stage a coup in 1992.' She noted that he had 'vowed to be inventive in tackling the country's problems, but promised no miracles or overnight solutions'. 'Serious leadership is needed,' he told the *Washington Post*, 'not irresponsible populism.'

Later in the year, Chávez set out to other parts of the world, including China, Japan, South Korea, Hong Kong, Malaysia, Singapore and the Philippines. Ever since the first presidency of Carlos Andrés Pérez in the 1970s, Venezuela had been counted among the nations of the Third World. Previous presidents, notably Pérez himself, had made a habit of visiting distant continents. Indeed, during his second presidency in the 1990s, Pérez was accused of spending too much time playing the role of international statesman. Yet Venezuela's position as a founder member of Opec obviously made it a world player, and Chávez, although inevitably busy at home, was well aware that he needed to secure as much international support as he could get.

In this context, his visit to China in October was of considerable importance, both politically and economically. Venezuela's potential need for rice and cheap consumer goods, and China's need for oil, made them complementary partners. But Chávez also liked the Chinese political position on world affairs. His enthusiasm for the 'third way' of the British prime minister, Tony Blair, had waned after the Kosovo war, when he understood that the British position of abject support for the United States was in direct opposition to his own view of how world affairs should be conducted.

Chávez told the Chinese leaders in Beijing that he was in favour of 'an open and multi-polar world' that would respect the sovereignty of peoples:

In Venezuela, far away in America, we have already raised the banner of popular sovereignty, and in that we are wholly in agreement with the people of China and their revolutionary government.

Paying a visit to the tomb of Mao Tse-tung on 12 October, he wrote a eulogy to which no one could take exception, to the 'great strategist, great soldier, great statesman, and great revolutionary'. And when he met the Chinese minister, Zhu Rongji, he said simply that Venezuela was beginning to 'stand up', just as China had 'stood up' fifty years earlier, 'under the leadership of its great helmsman'. Chávez told the Chinese that he did not believe in the neo-liberalism which had proved to be such a disaster in the Third World. It had tried to impose economic models from centres of world power in the West but had resulted in millions of people living in poverty, with only the prospect of unemployment, misery and death.

Soviet power has collapsed, but that does not mean that neo-liberal capitalism has to be the model followed by the peoples of the West. If only for that reason, we invite China to keep its flag flying, because this world cannot be run by a universal police force that seeks to control everything.

After travelling through Asia, Chávez returned home through Europe. He told the German prime minister, Gerhard Schröder, that he was hoping 'to create a different economic model', and that his advisers were 'looking with close attention at the German and European model'. He also said that the new constitution in Venezuela would give 'greater stability and security to national and foreign investment'.

But he also reverted to his emphasis on multi-polarity. The world should understand that 'a people had the right to reorganize its arrangements as it sees fit. There is a fundamental principle: the self determination of peoples. There cannot be an international politics that watches what other people are doing, and then imposes its own model.'

The enthusiasm of Chávez for a 'multi-polar' world still seems unusual in a Latin American context, although in the ten years since the end of the Cold War, the Europeans have frequently referred to its desirability. 'We cannot accept a politically unipolar world, nor the unilateralism of a single hyper-power,' announced the French foreign minister, Hubert Védrine, in a speech in Paris on 3 November. Yet in Latin America in the 1990s, the leading countries, notably Mexico and Argentina, and to a lesser extent Chile, have perceived themselves as members of 'the West', as potential members of the 'First World'. In their view, Latin America forms part of the American pole – an attitude not altogether different from that of Tony Blair in the United Kingdom. Yet even in the European debate, few people have indicated where other potential poles might be found. The United States and Europe are held up as unique examples.

Hugo Chávez takes an entirely different and innovative stand, lining up with Védrine in favour of multi-polarity, and making a specific bid for the formation of a Latin American pole. In this ambition he has the warm but tacit support of Brazil where President Fernando Henríque Cardoso, while happy to accept the American neo-liberal economic model, shares the traditional belief of successive Brazilian governments in the geo-political importance of a continental-size country like Brazil.

Chávez is optimistic about what he sees as a global renaissance of nationalism:

> I think we are living through a period in which nationalism is being re-born. You can see this in the conflict in Chechenia against the Russians. It's like the return of history, just as the old nations came back after the First World War . . .
>
> Before, there was a dual globalism, two imperial powers that wanted to gobble up the world, and then one of them collapsed and the other said, 'Now it's my turn, I am the owner of the new world order, the single power world'. Then that idea collapsed, and quite rapidly.
>
> What we have now is world disorder. There is no order, and there is not a single superpower. The future will have many centres, and we shall see the formation of alliances and blocks.

Chávez's problem is that there is no sign as yet of the countries of Latin America organizing themselves into a block capable of negotiating with the world outside the continent. It will take time for his message to percolate through. Many Latin American presidents will be reluctant to listen to it, for none of them has ever perceived Venezuela as a natural political leader in the continent.

In Venezuela, Chávez talks over the heads of his immediate listeners to the wider audience beyond. The same technique may well pay dividends in Latin America, and he will slowly gain an audience there too.

22

CIVIL WAR IN COLOMBIA: THE FUTURE OF THE BOLIVARIAN DREAM

I'm asking Chávez, please stay in your yard and we'll manage our own problems. We don't want to talk about the internal problems of Venezuela, because we don't want them to intervene in domestic issues in Colombia. If Chávez contacts the guerrillas, we want him to tell us first.

President Andrés Pastrana in Washington, September 1999

For the armed forces of Venezuela, and therefore for Hugo Chávez, the most stretching external problem facing the country – today, yesterday, and tomorrow – is its relationship with Colombia. Venezuela has hundreds of miles of unguarded borders with Colombia, a country involved for many decades in the kind of prolonged and vicious civil war that characterized Venezuela in the nineteenth century.

That war often spills over the frontier. Venezuelan land-owners in the states of Zulia and Táchira have been kidnapped on occasion, and lorry drivers taking goods in and out of Colombia have been attacked. Both sides in the war, the 'guerrillas' on the left and the 'paramilitaries' on the right, have been involved in these frontier incidents.

Yet the Colombian problem is far more significant and central to

Venezuela than the relatively simple issue of border incidents. Colombia is a country in a state of profound crisis, and the future of the Chávez government will inevitably be affected by what happens next door. The existing Colombian state is on the verge of collapse, indeed in much of the country it has already collapsed, undermined by the drugs economy that is now much larger than the traditional national economy.

More significantly, the new emerging forces in Colombia, associated with the Revolutionary Armed Forces of Colombia (the Farc) and the National Liberation Army (the ELN), express similar Bolivarian views to those of Hugo Chávez. There is today an identity of attitude between the Venezuelan government and the 'Farc government' that controls perhaps a third of Colombia. Officially, this common interest is disguised behind Venezuela's public desire, expressed to the 'official' government of President Andrés Pastrana in Bogotá, to assist in peace negotiations between the warring factions in Colombia. In reality, Hugo Chávez and his government are on the side of the Farc.

Chávez wants the Farc to win, or at any rate to be so successful in the peace negotiations that its incorporation into the government will entirely change the political complexion of Colombia. Were that to happen, Chávez's dream of recreating Gran Colombia – the old nineteenth-century alliance of Venezuela, Colombia and Ecuador, devised by Bolívar – would come true. The Bolivarian project that lies at the heart of his hopes for the continent would be well on its way.

The crisis in Colombia has been so prolonged, and has run through so many different phases, that anyone without a detailed knowledge of the country and its past finds it difficult to follow, let alone understand, what is going on. For most of its history Colombia has endured cycles of violence of extreme intensity. Much of this has been generated by peasant wars and struggles over land rights. The situation of civil war and local anarchy is so pronounced that the collapse of the central state has often been prophesied. Large swathes of this vast continent-sized country have never come under the control of the central government. In the past decade, the situation has altered significantly, partly because of the end of the Cold War and partly because of the changing nature of the drugs trade.

Manuel Marulanda, the Farc leader, is effectively the ruler of a third of the country. The ELN is not as large as the Farc, but it too has a capacity to mobilize and motivate a substantial slice of the population. Marulanda has been running great chunks of Colombia for nearly forty years, and now his guerrilla forces can pop up at any moment in almost any region. For most of that time, he was a peasant leader allied to the Colombian Communist Party. He took his orders from Jacobo Arenas, one of the most sophisticated Party theorists in Latin America. The peasant movement, for better or worse, was run by the Party – encouraged at some moments, switched off at others, according to the perceived political needs of the time.

Sometimes there were successes, as when the Party and the guerrillas of the Farc survived the attack on their base at Marquetalia in 1964, an attack launched by the Colombian army with United States assistance. Sometimes there were disasters, as occurred when the Party recommended the acceptance of peace offers and the establishment of a civilian front organization in the late 1980s, the Patriotic Union, that would participate in conventional politics. Many guerrilla leaders, from the Farc and other groups, descended from the hills to take part in the political campaigns of the Patriotic Union. The leaders, and thousands of their supporters, were promptly slaughtered by right-wing paramilitary groups. Plainly the policy had been an error. The experience had such an impact on Marulanda that to this day he is concerned that a peace agreement might lead to a repeat of the earlier catastrophe.

Although the Farc is at war with the Colombian army, their more formidable opponents are the paramilitary organizations. These are separate from the armed forces, though they often operate with their tacit support. Funded by the drug traffickers, they are immensely rich and powerful, and ruthless in war. The Farc also secures its financial support from the drug economy, though chiefly from the cultivators and the producers rather than the sellers and 'traffickers'. This may be a fine distinction, and there is at least one documented case of a Farc chieftain who funded his independent operation from the trade itself.

Since the destruction of the Patriotic Union, the situation is now rather different. The Farc is in a much more dominant position, obliging the government to come to the negotiating table. The Farc is not the same political animal as it was in earlier decades. With the collapse of the Soviet Union and the end of the Cold War there is no longer a powerful Communist Party capable of manipulating the peasant war. Jacobo Arenas, the *éminence grise* of the old Soviet-style Farc, has died. Manuel Marulanda has now returned to his previous incarnation as a traditional peasant leader operating on his own, conducting his war with peasant cunning and with forty years of accumulated experience behind him.

At the same time, the nature of the countryside, and of work in the countryside, has been changed out of all recognition, partly by the disruption and devastation of the war itself, and partly by the transformations in the drugs trade. For twenty years Colombia was a large producer of marihuana, the third largest in the Americas after the United States itself and Mexico, but it grew no poppies (mostly cultivated in Mexico and Guatemala), and it grew very little coca. Colombia merely processed the coca – grown in Peru and Bolivia – into cocaine, and exported it. Coca processing was not very labour-intensive.

Today the picture is rather different. The land devoted to growing cannabis, coca and poppy has grown five-fold. Colombia is now the second largest producer of coca in the Americas, and the largest exporter of heroin. The sums of money generated by this economic activity are so gigantic that the figures defy belief. According to one recent account, the drug traffickers, after twenty years in the business, had amassed a total of more than US$75 billion in 1997, more than Colombia's gross national product. Yet more significant, from the point of view of the peasant war, is the impact on rural employment.

Thousands more people work on plant production for drug use than twenty years ago, and they are seriously affected by indiscriminate drug eradication programmes.

In this context, the armed forces at the disposal of Marulanda are no longer small peasants fighting for their land, they are rural labourers fighting for their work. Marulanda has mobilized this rural proletariat that works the coca and marihuana plantations, and has defended them, with great success, against the efforts made to destroy their livelihood – by the government, the army, and the United States. Part of the reasons for the Farc's success is that Marulanda, too, has money to spend.

These developments are not just of interest to those concerned with the history of Colombia; they also have an impact on Venezuela. For part of Marulanda's 're-branding' of the Farc has involved a recovery of past history comparable to that undertaken by Hugo Chávez. The Colombian left, having escaped from the Marxist dislike for Bolívar espoused by the Communist Party, has begun to restore the figure of the Liberator to their pantheon of heroes. The Farc now have 'Bolivarian militias'. (Colombia, it should be said in passing, has always had some difficulty with Bolívar, since their very own hero of the time, Francisco de Paula Santander, was responsible for the breakup of the Bolivarian project of Gran Colombia.)

Nor is the Farc alone. Floating somewhere in the background are the former supporters of General Gustavo Rojas Pinilla, the dictator of the 1950s who ended the civil war of that time, the 'Violencia', and who now enjoys a recovered reputation not unlike that of Medina Angarita in Venezuela. When Rojas Pinilla attempted a come-back in the 1970s, he had considerable support from socialist nationalists of the kind who now give support to Hugo Chávez.

For the moment, the Chávez government has been content to follow in the footsteps of its predecessors in the 1990s, holding discussions about the border problem both with the government in Bogotá and with the guerrilla organizations. The minister for frontiers in the Caldera government was Pompeyo Márquez, a former Communist leader and an influential member of the Movimiento al Socialismo with a long-established relationship with Marulanda. He used his contacts to secure a promise from the Farc that they would not operate in Venezuelan territory. Other contacts with the Farc were made by Arias Cárdenas, the governor of the frontier state of Zulia, who has stated publicly that he believes the Colombian paramilitaries to be run by the Colombian army.

Former President Caldera had met the former Colombian president, Ernesto Samper, at the border town of Guasdualito in August 1997, and it was agreed that Venezuela should have a role in the projected peace negotiations which the Colombian government was about to hold with the guerrillas. These were organized at first by the Colombian congress and then taken up and given a new lease of life by the current President Andrés Pastrana. Venezuela subsequently suggested that Colombia should follow the Central American example and allow a 'Group of Friends' of the Colombian peace process to be formed, which Mexico, Costa Rica and Spain might also join.

President Chávez made clear at an early stage that he was anxious to continue this policy and to help with the peace process. Several members of his government have had informal contacts with the guerrilla movements, and meetings between guerrilla representatives and Venezuelan government officials have taken place both in Caracas and in Havana. While President Chávez has broadly followed the policies laid down by Caldera, Chávez himself and Arias Cardenas, and Foreign Minister Rangel, clearly lean more towards the Farc than to the regime in Bogotá.

In September 1999, President Pastrana began to express his concerns about Venezuela's intentions, as he explained to the *Washington Post*: 'I'm asking Chávez, please stay in your yard and we'll manage our own problems. We don't want to talk about the internal problems of Venezuela, because we don't want them to intervene in domestic issues in Colombia. If Chávez contacts the guerrillas, we want him to tell us first.'

Always hovering over these arguments between Caracas and Bogotá is the government in Washington. The United States has pledged itself to prop up the government in Bogotá at whatever the cost – and it has promised US$1.5 billion over the next three years. While it is obliged to pretend to support the Colombian peace talks, it would deplore any role for Farc supporters in a future Colombian government.

The United States military position in the area has been changed as a result of its treaty obligation to withdraw from its immense bases in the Panama Canal Zone, which were finally handed over to Panama in December 1999. American land, sea and air forces have all had to be relocated to other places, either in the United States itself or in the Caribbean. Since the United States now has access to airports in the Dutch Antilles, offshore from Venezuela, the Americans have been putting pressure on the Chávez government to allow them the right to overfly Venezuelan territory without prior permission while engaged in their campaign against the Colombian drugs trade.

Chávez, to the intense irritation of the Americans, has refused to allow them to do so. Since this policy of refusing permission is supported not just by the left but by the armed forces of Venezuela, the United States may have to admit that this is an argument they cannot win, although they have not given up trying to change Chávez's mind.

Just how powerful US pressure can be was revealed in January 2000 when Ecuador – the third element in Bolívar's Gran Colombia – looked for a moment as though it might follow in Venezuela's footsteps. An oil-rich but indebted country, with a rickety and incompetent *ancien régime*, Ecuador had announced its intention of adopting the US dollar as the national currency. The country's economy was in crisis, with inflation running at 60 per cent in 1999, and with more than half the population of 12 million living in absolute poverty. The dollarization strategy of President Jamil Mahuad was strenuously opposed by the country's large indigenous movement, representing an Indian population of more than 4 million, and by important sectors of the armed forces.

On Friday 23 January, after a march on the capital by thousands of Indians, young army officers led by Colonel Lucio Gutiérrez, and hundreds of Indians led by the principal indigenous leader, Antonio Vargas, seized the Congress building in Quito and announced the creation of a 'Parliament of the People'. On the following morning, Colonel Gutiérrez declared that the government of President Muhuad had been overthown and replaced by a three-man junta. Gutiérrez was to be one member of the junta, together with Vargas, a 40-year-old school-teacher and president of the National Confederation of Indigenous nations of Ecuador, and Carlos Solorzano, a former president of the Supreme Court. After some debate within the army, Gutiérrez was obliged to surrender his position on the junta to the commander-in-chief, General Carlos Mendoza.

The Ecuadorean military had been worried for some years about the capacity of the radicalized Indian movement to mobilize in the countryside, but was deeply divided about what should be done. Some reports suggested that Gutiérrez resigned in order to avoid a full-blown right-wing coup against the Indians. More than 20 regional commanders did not support the Gutiérrez/Vargas coup.

'Ecuador's Indian insurgency is one of the most dramatic phenomena to occur in recent years,' said General José Gallardo, the former defence minister, quoted in a despatch by Monte Hayes, the correspondent of the Associated Press in Quito. Gallardo, according to Hayes, had been 'the chief proponent within the armed forces of social assistance programmes in the early 1990s for rural Indian communities ignored by government agencies. The goal was to increase military influence in the villages and head off any threat to national security by a radicalized Indian movement.'

Later on Saturday 24 January, under extreme pressure from the US embassy in Quito, the morale of General Mendoza collapsed. He dissolved the junta, and, taking account of constitutional niceties, appointed the vice-president, Gustavo Noboa, as the new president. He told reporters that his decision was made after discussions with US officials, who had threatened to cut off foreign aid and investment if power was not restored to the elected government. 'We were trying to prevent the international isolation of Ecuador,' he said.

Solorzano and Vargas bitterly opposed the dissolution of the junta. Vargas denounced General Mendoza for betraying the Indians, and said that his federation would continue the struggle for radical change. The new government moved quickly against the coup organizers within the ranks of the military, arresting four colonels – Lucio Gutiérrez, Fausto Cobo, Gustavo Lalama and Jorge Brito – and 12 lieutenant colonels. Some 300 junior officers were also detained.

Ecuador is not Venezuela, and Colonel Gutiérrez is not Hugo Chávez. Ecuador has a deeply racist ruling elite, many of whose members will unite firmly against any threat to their privileges from the Indian underclass. Yet the coup attempt in January 2000 bears certain similarities with the Chávez coup of February 1992, and many believe that they have seen the writing on the wall for Ecuador's *ancien régime*.

23

NEW RIGHTS FOR
INDIGENOUS PEOPLES

If I was to choose a beautiful Venezuelan native, she would be an Indian, with a round face and rather short; so our philosophy is not to choose a Venezuelan beauty . . .

Osmel Sousa of the Miss Venezuela Organization

Venezuela produces more beautiful women than any other country in the world, according to the definitions of beauty created by the organizations that have devised the competitions for 'Miss World' and 'Miss Universe', yet none of the winners ever come from the indigenous peoples or the community of blacks.

If there is one single individual responsible for this state of affairs it must be Osmel Sousa, a former advertising designer who is the boss of the 'Miss Venezuela Organization'. He works from a small pink-washed villa in the centre of Caracas that serves both as an office and as a finishing school for aspiring beauties. Painted rose-pink inside as well as out, its lush interior might well be the setting for a Hollywood brothel. Here 26 young women come for five months every year to learn the finer points of deportment, style and presentation.

Señor Sousa sits behind a huge desk in a small room, framed by a huge and ornate full-length mirror. In the middle of the room is a tiny round pink-carpeted stage, where his potential pupils can display their attractions.

Sousa holds the franchise to operate the 'Miss Venezuela Organization' and he organizes an annual competition on Venezuelan television which presents the young women from his school. 'This programme has the largest rating of the entire year,' he says with some pride, 'so it's the most expensive. The sponsors have to pay a lot of money – and this finances our organization and our school.' His school has won the 'Miss Universe' and 'Miss World' competitions many times.

How does he spot the winners for his finishing school? 'I go to modelling schools and to fiestas as a kind of talent scout. We do a "casting" of 40 girls from which we choose ten. And then we go on until we've got 26. They then come here to the school and prepare for the competition. They come for five months. We show them how to prepare themselves, we teach them some phrases in English if they don't know it already. They learn how to do their hair and their make-up as though they were professionals, and they learn how to walk the catwalk. And of course they go to the gym, take exercise, and learn how to look after their bodies.'

In practice, the girls who come to the school are on a scholarship. 'They pay nothing. We only insist that they dedicate themselves to this full-time. They can't study or do anything else.'

Every year, there are 50 judges. 'They come from all strata of society,' Sousa claims, 'and they change every year. They are singers, actresses, politicians, hairdressers, designers, ex-beauty queens, diplomats. We have even had the British ambassador.' This is the organization that defines the nature of Venezuelan loveliness. How does he do it?

'Venezuelan beauty doesn't exist, for here there is a great mixture of races. If I was to choose a beautiful Venezuelan native, she would be an Indian, with a round face and rather short; so our philosophy is not to choose a Venezuelan beauty, but to select a young woman who was born in Venezuela. She could have a Hungarian father, a Spanish mother, anything, as long as she was born in Venezuela.'

What about blacks? Venezuela is a Caribbean country that once had a large slave population, and blacks still form a large minority in the coastal provinces. 'Yes, we have blacks,' says Sousa, and he leafs through a publicity brochure with the faces and figures of the previous years. 'Look, we always have a black. Here's one,' and he points to a picture of the pouting Miss Delta, one off-white face among a dozen full-blooded Aryans. 'She looks like Naomi Campbell, doesn't she?'

Yet there is a terrible truth to which he feels obliged to admit. 'Miss Venezuela has never been black.' And why should that be? 'Because the Venezuelan people would not perceive themselves to be well represented by a black.'

So long as the advertising industry goes on portraying white women in their advertisements, and so long as institutions like the Miss Venezuela Organization go on providing examples of white European beauty, this will almost certainly continue to be true.

What happens to Venezuela's former beauty queens, the ones that don't turn into presidential hopefuls like Irene Sáez? Sousa looks at his book of photographs. 'This one married a multi-millionaire. This one married a petrol magnate. This one was our third Miss World, she's an actress in America. This one works for a telephone company in the United States and earns lots of dollars. This one's a model in Italy.'

He leans back in his chair and reflects on the success of his charges. 'All of them come from the middle class and all of them marry very rich men. All of them have done very well, and we're very pleased. Rich girls in Venezuela have no desire to compete in beauty competitions. The rich have too much money.'

So just who are the Venezuelans? A million Europeans have come to settle in Venezuela in the years since 1945. Are they Venezuelans?

The Caribbean shores of the country throb to the rhythms of the progeny of former slaves from Africa. Are they Venezuelans?

More than 300,000 indigenous peoples live in the country's frontier provinces; in the forgotten areas of the states of Zulia and Táchira in the west, and in Amazonas and Bolívar to the south, live innumerable tribes and nations. Are they Venezuelans?

These are questions that 'the Venezuelans' rarely seem to ask themselves. For decades they have mouthed nationalist slogans and bowed down silently before the image of Columbus and Simón Bolívar, yet they do not ask themselves who they are or where they came from. This is the challenge facing the government of President Chávez, and he does not shrink from it: 'History is not a single epic tale,' he told Agustín Blanco Muñoz, 'it is the history of culture, how the country was created, why we are the colour we are, why the country is called Venezuela, what was the process that brought us to where we are now.' In 1999, during the meetings of the new Constituent Assembly, some of these questions about national identity began to be asked. The most heated discussions concerned the rights to be granted to the country's indigenous peoples in the new constitution.

Out of Venezuela's population of 23 million, some 316,000 (about 1.4 per cent) are identified as indigenous peoples, although the number is almost certainly much larger. The most numerous group, the Wayúu, also known as the Guajíra, probably total about 197,000 and live chiefly in the state of Zulia, between Lake Maracaibo and the Colombian border.

In the half empty areas of the east and the south live another 100,000 indigenous people: 44,000 in Amazonas, 35,000 in Bolívar, and 21,000 in Delta Amacuro. To the north of the Orinoco, 7,000 live in Anzoátegui, and 6,000 in Apure.

Some 26 different ethnic groups are believed to live in Venezuela and they have been given many names by settlers over the centuries. They deserve to be described by the names that they give themselves: Wayúu, Warao, Pemón, Añú, Yanomani, Jivi, Piaroa, Kariña, Pumé, Yecuana, Yukpa, Eñepá, Kurripakao, Barí, Piapoko, Baré, Baniva, Puinave, Yeral, Jodi, Kariná, Warekena, Yarabana, Sapé, Wanai, Uruak.

The Chávez government has taken a fresh interest in the future of the indigenous peoples from the start. Atala Uriana, a Wayúu leader from Zulia, and a supporter of the Polo Patriótico, was appointed as the first minister of the environment, though he later resigned to become a member of the Constituent Assembly. In the run-up to the elections to the Assembly, special arrangements were made to ensure the election of at least three representatives of the indigenous peoples. Conive, the National Council of Indigenous Peoples, held a conference in March to choose their delegates: Nohelí Pocaterra, a Wayúu, and a social worker and the president of the World Council of Indigenous Peoples; José Luís González, a Pemón, and a sociologist, a prominent member of Conive and the founder of the Asociación Indígena in Bolívar state; and Guillermo Guevara, a Jivi, and the director of the Organización Regional de los Pueblos Indígenos of Amazonas state. All had long experience of promoting the rights of indigenous peoples.

The history of white settlement and indigenous resistance in Venezuela is long, complicated, and under-researched, though what has long been clear is that independence in the early nineteenth century made matters worse for the indigenous peoples. For two centuries the Spaniards permitted the Capuchins, the Jesuits and the Franciscans to organize mission stations, and the Indians there enjoyed some measure of protection. But the Jesuits withdrew in the 1760s, and a more violent fate awaited the Capuchins half a century later. Their extensive missions along the Caroní river had been planted close to the Orinoco delta for strategic reasons, for they helped to guard the country against the English and the Dutch. In 1817 they were affected by the arrival of the forces of Bolívar, who realized that whosoever controlled the rich Capuchin missions would win the war. The missionaries, like most of the Catholic Church, had chosen to side with the Spanish, and on 7 May 1817, they suffered for their choice. Twenty missionaries, aged between 32 and 70, were slaughtered. The troops of the Liberator seized the missions, stole their grain and cattle, and enrolled the mission Indians into their regiments.

Throughout the nineteenth century, successive governments had no policy for the indigenous peoples other than a vain hope that the old missions might be restored. The Indians were driven relentlessly out from the centre towards the frontiers of the state.

Further to the south, in the middle of the eighteenth century, the

Spanish had begun pushing up into the waters of the Upper Orinoco. The Yecuana, then known as the Makiritare, did not care for the new arrivals, and for several years, between 1765 and 1775, they organized a serious resistance campaign. On a single night at the end of 1775, they captured and burnt down 19 Spanish forts and camps along the road constructed from Angostura (Ciudad Bolívar) to La Esmeralda on the Upper Orinoco.

More than 100 years later, in May 1913, during the rubber boom, the whites hit back. Colonel Tomás Fúnes seized control of San Fernando de Atabapo with a small force of rubber workers, and the town's governor, Roberto Pulido, was killed, as were his wife and brothers and 130 settlers. It was but a preliminary to the slaughter of the Makiritare Indians. Colonel Fúnes controlled the town for nine years, far beyond the control of the central state, and killed Indians on a massive scale. A book called 'Los Hijos de la Luna' describes how 'dozens and dozens of Makiritares villages were destroyed and their inhabitants killed. At a rough calculation, two thousand Indians were slaughtered during those tragic years . . .'

Colonel Fúnes surrendered in 1921 to the forces of General Emilio Arévalo Cedeño, a famous anti-Gómez guerrilla leader allied with Maisanta, the great-grandfather of President Chávez. Fúnes foolishly believed that he had surrendered in return for his life, but he was shot anyway. The indigenous peoples of Venezuela remember the stories of their oppression with greater detail than do the heirs of the white settlers.

In October 1999, Pemón Indians living in the south-east corner of Venezuela drew attention to their presence by destroying a number of electricity pylons. The pylons had been constructed across their territory to conduct a high-voltage line from the Guri dam to Brazil. The Pemón disliked the pylons, and claimed that the easy availability of cheap electricity would only encourage further development by mining companies. The gold deposits in the region had already attracted an army of labourers with scant respect for the rights of the Pemón. The government's official position was that the pylons would inflict little environmental damage; development of the region was needed in order to create jobs. The electricity project, costing US$110 million, could not be stopped since contracts had already been signed with towns in northern Brazil.

In December, one of the great indigenous leaders of Latin America, Rigoberta Menchú, arrived in Caracas to give her blessing to the changes relating to indigenous rights published in the new constitution. Rigoberta, from Guatemala, won the Nobel Peace Prize in 1992. She has been a tireless protagonist in the continental campaign to secure the recognition of the rights of indigenous peoples:

> In many countries they have been discussing these questions during the last 15 or 20 years, and they have imagined that to give rights to indigenous people might be a bad thing, or might affect adversely the rest of the citizenry, But we have shown that we are patriots; that's where we stand, even if we have been affected by racism and exclusion . . . It's important that people should abandon these fantasies, for they are a shackle on the development of peaceful coexistence between different groups.

White-settler attitudes towards indigenous peoples have been changing in recent years all over the Americas. In some countries, the indigenous people are the majority of the population and are beginning to glimpse the power which is their due. Elsewhere the *mestizos*, those of mixed race, are beginning, like the blacks, to wonder how to define themselves in new and changing situations. These will become important debates in the twenty-first century, and Venezuela under Chávez is one of the vanguard countries where these issues are being brought out into the open.

24

TEODORO PETKOFF AND
THE OPPOSITION TO CHÁVEZ

The overwhelming defeat of the traditional parties in the elections at the end of 1998, and their notable lack of support or affection in the hearts and minds of the great mass of the people, has meant the complete collapse of any organized political opposition to Chávez.

Every afternoon in Caracas, concerned and politically aware citizens make a special effort to go out to buy *El Mundo*, the evening newspaper published by the Capriles group and edited, throughout 1999, with great flair and brilliance by Teodoro Petkoff. *El Mundo* has been the intelligent face of opposition to Hugo Chávez. Accurate, informed and intensely irritating, it speaks its mind with immense vitality.

Teodoro Petkoff, like so many participants in the Venezuelan drama, is a guerrilla fighter of yesteryear. Born in 1931, the son of immigrants from Bulgaria who had settled near Maracaibo, Petkoff joined the youth movement of the Communist Party in 1949, at the start of the Pérez Jiménez dictatorship. Although he studied to be a doctor like his mother, he was soon drawn to political activism and to journalism. In the Party's central committee in 1961, he was a keen advocate of armed revolt against the government of Rómulo Betancourt, and in 1962 he followed Douglas Bravo into the hills. Twice detained, he was held in the San Carlos prison in Caracas for three years, from 1964 to 1967, when he took part with others in a spectacular escape.

Petkoff has been a permanent dissident. He grew increasingly unhappy with the strategy taken by the Communist Party, and was an early critic of the Soviet invasion of Czechoslovakia in 1968, an event supported both by the Party and by Fidel Castro. In 1969, he accepted the offer made to the guerrillas by President Rafael Caldera to come down from the hills, or to return from exile, and in 1970 he helped to set up the Movimiento al Socialismo that split off from the Communist Party.

During the subsequent thirty years, Petkoff has been the conscience of the ever-squabbling Venezuelan left. A euro-communist *avant la lettre*, he was their presidential candidate on several occasions. In the 1990s, as the crisis of Venezuelan society became ever more grave, he put his name and his credibility, and his immense energy and talent, at the service of President Caldera, the octogenarian Kerensky of the *ancien régime*. As Caldera's minister of development, Petkoff gave this last gasp government the capacity to survive. It was a typically courageous gesture.

Then, in the middle of 1998, when the leaders of the political vehicle that Petkoff had helped to create some thirty years earlier decided to harness its strength to the presidential campaign of Hugo Chávez, Petkoff jumped off. His resignation from the MAS was a defining moment for the left. Some remained with Chávez, others became columnists on *El Mundo*, the paper Petkoff now took over to propagate his own political position against that of Chávez.

For most of the first year of the Chávez government, the columnists of *El Mundo* and the other newspapers, particularly *El Universal*, fearlessly put their heads above the parapet and sniped away at the new policies. Rather surprisingly for a government with so many journalists in it, the Chávez regime proved notably poor at public relations and was wholly unable to rebut the attacks of the hostile press. The columnists, drawn up and orchestrated by Petkoff, made a formidable noise; yet they were voices crying in the wilderness, quite without political backing. When Petkoff was forced to resign as editor by the owners of the paper, apparently for commercial reasons, their weakness was revealed. The overwhelming defeat of the traditional parties in the elections at the end of 1998, and their notable lack of support or affection in the hearts and minds of the great mass of the people, has meant the complete collapse of any organized political opposition to Chávez. Such is the discredit into which yesterday's politicians have fallen that most of them have crept away or stayed at home to write their memoirs.

The only serious opposition, apart from the columnists, has come from the leaders of the once powerful economic groups, traditionally accustomed to sounding off and being listened to: men like Vicente Brito, the president of Fedecamaras; Antonio Herrera Vaillant, the vice-president of the all-embracing Venamcham, the Venezuelan–American chamber of commerce which groups together a thousand foreign and national businesses; and Luís Eduardo Paul, the president of the Cámara Petrolera. Notably during the debates about the new constitution, these individuals and their groups took it upon themselves, through interviews and press conferences, to outline their opposition to the economic clauses that appeared to adversely affect their interests. Yet they, as well as the columnists, were without significant political backing.

Occasionally, a voice from the former era can be heard. Many old conservatives fear what they call the 'neo-populism' of Chávez. Eduardo Fernández, once a presidential hopeful of Copei, denounced 'the messianism, the paternalism, the centralism, and the rentier vision of the economy' that he believes to be sweeping Venezuela and Latin America, with 'apathetic and depoliticized masses' rising above the old parties and ideologies.

Towards the end of 1999, during the referendum campaign for the new constitution, this opposition became increasingly shrill, clothing itself in the traditional garb of the Latin American right. Fears were expressed that democracy was in the process of being destroyed by democratic means. Chávez was attacked as a long-term 'conspirator' and criticized for his use of violent language, 'the language of civil war'. The opposition complained that the customary civilities of debate were being abandoned, with 'the country split in two halves that do not speak to each other'.

Much of the overblown rhetoric of this embryonic opposition was designed to summon up various potential opponents to Chávez to join a new political crusade against him. Chávez, it was claimed, was against the political parties, against the business community, against the media, and hostile to the Catholic Church. If these sectors of society would only wake up to the menace that he posed, then a new political movement of opposition might be organized.

Some critics have even gone so far as to suggest that sections of the military are unhappy with the Chávez project and might be willing to listen to subversive talk of a new coup. There are people in Chávez's old Bolivarian Revolutionary Movement who are unhappy about the way things are going. Some are conservative, but others want government policies to be more revolutionary, not less. They want action against the rich and privileged, and a firmer defence of Venezuelan interests against the United States. And, as must be obvious from the details in this book, organizing a military coup is not an everyday event that any disgruntled officer can stage. Even when planned by men of competence and vision, with popular support, it can very easily fail.

Yet one day an opposition will certainly appear. Many of the old politicians hope that their discredited parties will arise once again. This is what happened in General Velasco's Peru and General Perón's Argentina, where the old parties sprang back into action when the interregnum was over. Yet Venezuela appears to be going through a more profound upheaval, one that will leave the political landscape changed for ever. When a Venezuelan civilian opposition does finally emerge, it will come from within the ranks of the *chavistas*, from people unhappy about the speed of change.

In January 2000, as the government came up to its first anniversary, signs of serious trouble emerged among the old *chavistas*. Chávez was already in the process of reorganizing his cabinet, but before he could do so he was obliged to accept the resignation of Colonel Jesús Urdaneta, the head of the Disip, the secret police, and one of his closest and oldest military colleagues.

The original cause of Urdaneta's surprise departure was his refusal to prepare a report, requested by Chávez, on the activities of Disip operatives during the episodes of looting that had occurred after the mudslides in December. Press reports had revealed instances of looters being shot, and although the president initially denied that anything untoward had occurred, he was urged by José Vicente Rangel to ask Urdaneta for a detailed report. As foreign minister, Rangel was aware of the pressures from abroad, and from potential aid donors, and he knew of the harm that the reports of the execution of looters were causing.

Urdaneta, as the intelligence chief, had a shrewd idea about what had gone on, but he told Chávez that he could only provide a general account not a detailed one, since he needed 'to protect' his men. By way of a counter-attack, he asked the president what he had done with an earlier Disip report that had detailed alleged instances of corruption committed by Rangel and Luís Miquilena. For the first time, Chávez was faced with a decision about the relative merits of the civilian and the military wings of his government.

Faced with such obvious blackmail, Chávez had no difficulty in coming down on the side of the civilians. He is reported to have put his hand on Urdaneta's shoulder, and said: 'Brother, I don't think we're going to come to an agreement that way.' Urdaneta was immediately sacked, and replaced at Disip by another Chávez loyalist, Captain Eliézer Otaiza.

Within the week, Chávez had made a major reshuffle of his senior colleagues, appointing a civilian, Isaías Rodríguez, to the new post of vice-president, and sending Ignácio Arcaya back to his old job at the United Nations in New York, and replacing him as interior minister by Luís Alfonso Dávila. A new minister of defence was also appointed, General Ismail Eliézer Hurtado, replacing General Raúl Sálazar.

Captain Otaiza began an investigation into the activities of the Disip agents who had been operating in the mudslide areas. This was no easy task since the Disip, being a secret police force, had operatives who used pseudonyms and were accustomed to protecting each other against outside criticism. Otaiza was eventually obliged to call in DIM, the military intelligence, to speed up the investigation.

Early the following month, on Friday 4 February, large demonstrations were held in towns all over the country to celebrate the eighth anniversary of the Chávez 'military intervention' of 1992. Chávez himself spoke in Caracas, saying that he still felt that 'it was worth it'.

Elsewhere, however, further trouble was brewing, for Colonel Urdaneta had no intention of disappearing quietly into history. He teamed up with two of Chávez's oldest colleagues in the Bolivarian movement, Colonel Arias Cárdenas, the influential governor of Zulia, and Colonel Yoel Acosta Chirinos, the organizer of the Fifth Republic Movement. On the same Friday, the three officers staged their own celebrations in the historically significant city of Coro, issuing a statement accusing the government of losing its way. Coro, the capital of Falcón state, was close to the coast and had often been the launching pad for opposition movements in the nineteenth century.

The chief complaint of the three officers was that their military revolution had been hijacked by the civilians. Urdaneta now launched a bitter campaign of criticism against the two principal civilians supporting Chávez, Miquilena and Rangel. Chávez appeared on television to express his sadness at this turn of events, and thanked Urdaneta and his other former comrades for their work over the years. But he explained that the process had moved on. They were no longer a small group of conspirators, but a government with responsibilities to the nation as a whole.

The newspapers made much of the divisions in the ranks of the former *comandantes*, and even raised the possibility of a military coup. Yet in practice, Chávez remained firmly in command, and in any case Arias Cárdenas and Acosta Chirinos were by no means as outspokenly critical as Urdaneta Hernández. It was not difficult to drive a wedge between them. The charges of corruption against Miquilena and Rangel, raised by Urdaneta, were easily dismissed.

The real cause of the trouble was the forthcoming elections, scheduled for 28 May, and the struggle within the Fifth Republic Movement for the spoils. Many jobs were on offer, for state governors and mayors, but there were too many candidates for too few positions. Members of the Movement, and members of the constituent parts of the Polo Patriótico, were all anxious to receive the presidential nod.

Miquilena, as the principal political brain in control of the Fifth Republic Movement, was the key figure. He made all the decisions about individual advancement, and ensured that a balance was kept between the civilians and the military, and between left and right. As such, he was detested by those he had slighted or put down. Yet since he had the ear of the president, for Chávez recognized that he was the most indispensable figure in his government, his opponents on this occasion were easily outmanoeuvred.

Arias Cárdenas was eventually persuaded to throw his hat into the ring, and to stand as a presidential candidate against Chávez in the May elections. Although an intelligent man, with considerable local support in Zulia, it never seemed likely that he could achieve the degree of national popularity accorded to Chávez.

In the longer term, the problem of the formation of a constitutional and respected opposition remains unsolved. It is clearly unsatisfactory to have a hostile and irresponsible press, operating at the whim of its rich owners, while many of the old group of officers who formed the initial support for the Chávez intervention are still wedded to dreams of unconstitutional action. The discredited political parties of the *ancien régime* show no sign of recovering their earlier strength. Only after the May elections will it be possible to discern the shape and size of future opposition forces.

EPILOGUE: THE MILITARY AND CIVIL SOCIETY

> The idea is to return the military to their basic social function, so that both as citizens and as an institution, they can be incorporated into the democratic development projects of the country.
>
> Hugo Chávez, interviewed in January 2000

President Chávez is interested in education and in economic development, yet he is first and foremost a soldier. Two of the historical figures that he has placed on a pedestal, Bolívar himself and Ezequiel Zamora, are unambiguously military. 'I understand the soul of the army,' he told me during our conversation at La Casona, 'and I am part of that soul.' One of his most controversial ambitions is to integrate the armed forces into the life of civil society.

For many people outside Latin America, particularly in the quarter of a century since General Augusto Pinochet overthrew Salvador Allende in September 1973, it is almost impossible to think of a military leader without conjuring up the grotesque image of a junta in dark glasses presiding over an authoritarian and repressive regime. Few recall the handful of radical military rulers who have taken the side of the peasantry and pushed through radical reforms in the teeth of fierce opposition from local oligarchs and the United States. Few remember that Allende recruited radical officers to serve in his government.

Chávez knows well that many people, in Latin America and beyond, are often reticent about supporting a government with influential military participation, even when democratically elected. He explains how shocked his generation of soldiers was at the Chilean coup, yet he is also keen to reveal how impressed they all were by the progressive military governments of Peru and Panama. Chávez is proud of his military antecedents, and he believes firmly that soldiers have a right to be brought out into society, and should not be permanently banished to their barracks. He wants to see a revolution in the relationship between the military and the civilian sectors of society, and he is pleased that soldiers now have a right to vote.

As José Vicente Rangel explained to me:

> Chávez is part of an atypical generation of officers. They emerged in the period when the Venezuelan army was coming out of the guerrilla struggle of the 1960s. During that time the army – and all the armies of the region – had been 'Pentagonized'. The US School of the Americas in Panama, and the US military 'advisers', and the 'national security doctrine', all played an important role.

Then, once the guerrilla phenomenon had disappeared in the 1970s, 'the officers began to search for new motivations. They started to study in the universities, and made connections with civil society.' As the economic and social situation in the country got worse, 'the officers who were no longer cooped up in the ghetto of the barracks began to experience the social crisis at first hand'.

They were affected by an additional and decisive factor.

> Corruption had a rather special impact on the armed forces. A large part of the officer corps was involved in it. I think they may have been encouraged in this by the civilian political leadership, which may have thought that corrupting the senior officers would

guarantee their support and neutralize their discontent. This may have neutralized the top echelons, but it created great discontent further down, among officers who were studying and had contact with students. They began to notice that the senior officers were taking part in a bonanza, and that some of them were enriching themselves very rapidly.

When I discussed this with Chávez at La Casona, he emphasized the humiliation suffered by the junior officers of his generation.

The lack of balance in the country affected the military. At one extreme of the pendulum were the *gorilas*, at the other extreme the eunuchs. Over many years the Venezuelan military have been eunuchs: we were not allowed to speak, we had to look on in silence while we watched the disaster being caused by corrupt and incompetent governments. Our senior officers were stealing, our troops were eating almost nothing, and we had to remain under tight discipline. But what kind of discipline was that? It was being complicit with the disaster.

Chávez wants to bring the military into civil society, 'but not as *gorilas*, not as Hitler or Mussolini, no, none of that. The idea is to return the military to their basic social function, so that both as citizens and as an institution, they can be incorporated into the democratic development projects of the country.'

During the first year of the Chávez government, the military worked on its own democratic social project, called the 'Plan Bolívar 2000'. 'Thank goodness we had had the experience of the Plan Bolívar,' Chávez told me. 'We had been working on it for ten months in the coastal area, and it was just as well, for the military had become sensitized to these issues. They had already been working in what was to be the disaster zone on humanitarian tasks; it didn't cost us anything to use this huge human potential to help in the task of rescuing people and saving lives.'

He recognizes that the military are now going further, 'incorporating themselves, little by little, into the political leadership of the country, but not into *party* politics'. Chávez is bitterly hostile to the two political parties that have dominated the country for so many years, and he does not really like political parties at all, a notion that he has acquired partly from the theorists of La Causa Radical, who have developed an ideology similar to that of the German Greens. His own party, the Fifth Republic Movement, is a fairly moribund affair, and the two principal parties that support him, the Movement to Socialism and the Fatherland for All (a split from La Causa Radical), are forever squabbling.

Chávez is also keen for the military to promote a modest internationalism.

> They go to the United States, but they also go to Cuba, to Bolivia, and to Brazil, to explain the Plan Bolívar. They explain to people that the Venezuelan armed forces now have a social function. After all, we're not thinking of going to war with anyone, not with Colombia, not with Brazil, not with Guayana, or with Cuba, or with anyone.

Ecuador is one country where the Chávez message has been heard loud and clear, and in January radical officers united with the peasants from the Andes in an attempt to overthrow the government.

Reporters have always been susceptible to the charms of Latin America's radical strongmen, and I am no exception. Graham Greene fell in love with the late General Omar Torríjos, the left-wing ruler of Panama who persuaded Jimmy Carter to hand over the Panama Canal, and is one of Chávez's models. Gabriel García Márquez has never disguised his affection for Fidel Castro, another of Chávez's heroes; while many Peruvian intellectuals were hypnotized by the late General Juan Velasco, who pioneered 'the military road to socialism' in the 1960s – an example that Chávez also cherishes. Hugo Chávez has the same magnetic charisma as his predecessors, but he is an attractive and audacious colonel with a difference: his unsuccessful attempt to seize power by force was subsequently ratified by a grateful people at a presidential election.

Chávez's enthusiasm for change is infectious. His search for an alternative to the life of the shanty town is highly ambitious, for Venezuela is still a society of gangsters and looters – as the reports of the December disaster made plain. In their unruly behaviour, the young in the shanty towns are only following the example of their elders and betters in the more rarefied spheres of the nation, who have robbed and looted the country's wealth on an unprecedented scale.

To turn these amoral people living on their wits into selfless pioneers going out to make the desert bloom will require a large dose of imagination and a huge leap of faith. The guinea pigs for his experiment, the people whose houses have been swept away by the floods, will not find the choice an easy one. Would you rather live in a shanty town overlooking the Caribbean which falls into the sea every twenty years, or would you rather move to the distant shores of the Orinoco, filled with unpleasant insects and diseases, that has never before in history supported a large population? Would you rather be in a Caracas slum, surrounded by friends and neighbours, with the possibility of selling oddments on the streets, or would you like to go somewhere in the country where a benevolent government might provide you with a home, and eventually with land and work? These are real and difficult choices.

The revolutionary programme of the Chávez government is suffused with these utopian aspirations, and much has still to be spelt out. Yet he has issued a new prospectus for development in South America, and one with implications for Washington as well. For his hostility to neo-liberalism and globalization, his support for the rights of indigenous peoples, and his search for an agricultural strategy that would allow his country to feed its own people all combine to put him in tacit alliance with the protesters in Seattle in November 1999 at the conference of the World Trade Organization. Globalization may be the disease of the new millennium, but antibodies to combat it are slowly being created.

Radical leaders in Latin America tend to come to a sticky end. Free elections have sometimes turned up winners who are too far to the left to be easily countenanced by governments in Washington. Successive American governments have had innumerable arrows in their quiver for destroying regimes of which they disapprove, ranging from assassination or military invasion, through to the financing of opposition groups, and the manipulation of hostile press campaigns, to outright destabilization by political and economic means.

The Americans have been unusually silent about Chávez, and even the local conservative opposition, so used to taking its cue from Washington, has confined its activities to vindictive articles in the Caracas press. The Americans, preoccupied with presidential elections, and principally concerned with the outcome of the civil war in Colombia – and now with events in Ecuador – have still not decided what to think about Chávez. The Venezuelan opposition knows exactly what it thinks, but it has been so battered by the complete collapse of the *ancien régime*, and is so definitively rejected and unloved, that it shows no signs of an early recovery.

What, then, are we to make of Hugo Chávez? Is he a democrat, or a dictator in the making? Is he an anachronistic throw-back, advocating the failed economic and political recipes of yesteryear? Or does he represent a possible future for Latin America, a genuine alternative to globalization and neo-liberalism?

I perceive him to be an interesting and significant figure, an honest man with the interests of his people at heart, who hopes to change the history of his nation for the better. He will not turn out to be a Mussolini, nor is he the dangerous Bonapartist once so brilliantly evoked by Marx. Chávez will remain a man of the left, a radical searching for new forms of politics, new structures of economic organization, and different ways of perceiving the future of international relations within Latin America, and between the two Americas.

Clearly he has a utopian vision, not uncommon in a continent from which utopias are believed to spring, and in the nature of things it would be foolish not to imagine that his dreams will eventually be betrayed. Yet he has summoned some of the best people in the country to his side, and within a year he has disposed of the cadavers of the old political parties and laid down the framework for a recovery of the history of Venezuela that may eventually lead to a cultural revival capable of resisting the 'colossus of the North'.

With an intelligent and discriminating attitude towards the politics of oil, and with a powerful rhetoric directed towards the excesses of neo-liberalism, he may yet get the economy of Venezuela moving again, in a manner beneficial to the bulk of its impoverished population, most of whom have missed out on the advances of the twentieth century. Maybe this won't happen. Maybe it will all end in tears. Many radical projects in Latin America have been left, like corpses on a gibbet, to turn and twist in the wind. The proposals of Comandante Chávez deserve a better fate.

APPENDIX A

THE RIGHTS OF INDIGENOUS PEOPLES

The articles of the Venezuelan constitution of December 1999 regarding the rights of indigenous peoples:

Chapter VIII

Article 119

The State recognizes the existence of the indigenous peoples and communities, their social, political and economic organization, their cultures, their customs and practices, languages and religions, as well as their habitat and native rights to the lands which they ancestrally and traditionally occupy and which are necessary to develop and guarantee their way of life. It is the role of the State, with the participation of the indigenous peoples, to demarcate and guarantee the right to the collective ownership of the same, which shall be inalienable, imprescriptible, non-sequestrable and non-transferable under the terms of the Constitution and the law.

Article 120

The exploitation by the State of natural resources in indigenous areas shall be carried out without harm to the cultural, social and economic integrity of the same, and is subject to prior warning and consultation of the respective indigenous communities. The benefits accruing to the indigenous peoples from this exploitation shall be in accordance with the Constitution and the law.

Article 121

The indigenous people have the right to maintain and develop their ethnic and cultural identity, as well as their cosmology, values and spirituality and their sacred sites and forms of worship. The State will promote respect for and dissemination of the cultural products of the indigenous peoples, who have the right to their own form of education and to a multicultural and bilingual educational regime which reflects their own socio-cultural characteristics, values and traditions.

Article 122

The indigenous peoples have the right to an integral health [service] which takes into account their practices and cultures. The State recognizes their traditional medicine and complementary therapies, in accordance with bio-ethical principles.

Article 123

The indigenous peoples have the right to maintain and promote their own economic practices, based on reciprocity, solidarity and exchange, their traditional productive activities and their participation in the national economy, and to define their priorities. The indigenous peoples have the right to professional training services and to participate in the drafting and execution of specific programmes of training, technical and financial assistance services which strengthen their economic activities within the framework of local sustainable development.

Article 124

The collective intellectual property of the indigenous peoples in regard to their technological knowledge and innovations is guaranteed. Every activity relating to genetic resources and the knowledge associated with the same will be for [their] collective benefit. The patenting of ancestral resources and knowledge is forbidden.

Article 125

The indigenous peoples have the right to political participation. The State shall guarantee indigenous representation in the National Assembly and in the deliberative bodies of federal and local entities with an indigenous population, in accordance with the law.

Article 126

The indigenous peoples as cultures with ancestral roots form part of the Venezuelan nation, State and people, unique, sovereign and indivisible, and under the terms of this Constitution have a duty to safeguard the integrity and sovereignty of the nation.

The term 'people' should not be interpreted as having any implications in regard to the rights that this term may confer under International Law.

APPENDIX B

SAUCE OF WONDER

Richard Gott relishes a strange connection between Worcestershire and Venezuela

Reprinted from *The Guardian* (London), 11 December 1976

At the turn of the century in Caracas, after an outside concert by the band, the European-oriented Venezuelan gentry would repair for a social cup of chocolate, then one of the country's chief products, to 'La India', the Caracas equivalent of Sacher's or Demel's in Vienna. Nowadays 'La India' is a company, not a coffee house, the Venezuelan subsidiary of the General Foods Corporation, a powerful US transnational company. Its manager, Bill MacClarence, is a graduate of the Harvard Business School and has been with General Foods for 25 years.

Among the foods he produces for the discriminating palate of the Venezuelan middle class is *Salsa Inglesa* – English sauce. On the strangely familiar label it proclaims defiantly and unpronounceably in Spanish, 'Worcestershire Sauce'. The label itself is familiar because it says 'Lea and Perrins, the original and genuine'. The sauce in fact is made under licence in Venezuela by an American company that pays royalties to the British firm in Worcestershire, contributing doubtless to the 'invisibles' that keep Britain afloat.

Now if there is one thing that the countries of Latin America do not lack it is the wherewithal and the traditional skill to make an immense variety of sauces, chutneys and condiments. Hot and salt, sweet and savoury, the material is there – red peppers, green peppers, chili peppers, mangoes, plantain and ají. A cuisine cultivated, protected and enriched through the centuries by an oppressed but resourceful peasantry. So it comes as some surprise that there should be such a large demand in Venezuela for Lea and Perrins.

But look along the shelves of a suburban supermarket in Caracas and there is another bottle of *Salsa Inglesa*, 'French's Worcestershire Sauce', made this time by a British company, Reckitt's and Colman of Hull. It has a Venezuelan subsidiary, Atlantic Venezolana, which makes Worcestershire Sauce under licence from the H.T. French Company of Rochester in the United States – a British company manufacturing Worcestershire Sauce in Venezuela and paying royalties to an American company for the privilege of doing so. Atlantic Venezolana, perhaps to the delight of the Venezuelan housewife, also makes Brasso, Robinson's Barley Water, and Cherry Blossom shoe polish.

Two companies making Worcestershire Sauce in Venezuela might seem one too many, but not of course to those who dislike monopolies and extol the virtues of competition. And competition there certainly is. Further along the supermarket shelf stands yet another brand, 'McCormick's Worcestershire Sauce', made by McCormick de Venezuela, a subsidiary of the McCormick Company of Baltimore, manufactured under licence from nobody. The boss of McCormick de Venezuela, Manuel Mosteiro Pérez, is a Cuban exile who used to sell the company's sauce and mayonnaise in Havana. The revolution put paid to that. The Cuban subsidiary was confiscated. Now he flogs the stuff all over Latin America.

Nor does the story end here. Also on sale is 'Royal Worcestershire Sauce' (perhaps to be eaten off Royal Worcester dishes), produced by a subsidiary of Standard Brands. The president of the Venezuelan company is Eduardo Pinilla Pocaterra. As the name implies, he has little land – but his family owns plenty of banks. He did a spell at the University of New York's Graduate School of Business, where clearly he learned to put the Venezuelan taste for Worcestershire Sauce to profitable ends.

Heinz, 'the one you love', has also launched a Worcestershire Sauce onto the Venezuelan market. The boss of Alimentos Heinz de Venezuela, Louis Pacini, hails from Massachusetts, and used to be an operations officer in the US Army's Counter-Intelligence Corps in France and Austria in the 1950s. Now he just sells food.

So, five brands of Worcestershire Sauce are sold in Venezuela, mostly by American companies. A basic component of most of them, the soya bean, has to be imported. Venezuela can no longer feed itself and has a massive annual import bill for food. The companies that benefit are American: Kraft, Kellogg, Del Monte, Great Plains Wheat de Venezuela (cables: USWHEAT), National Biscuit and Quaker. They, and many more, are well established in Venezuela, though they don't make Worcestershire Sauce.

What about Nelson Rockefeller, the American who seems to control much of Latin America? Well, he owns the supermarket. Or at least he did until Carlos Andrés Pérez, the Venezuelan president, decided to nationalize it. How about nationalizing Lea and Perrins? It wouldn't be difficult to give it a new name: Lea and Pérez.

BIBLIOGRAPHY

Arvelo Ramos, Alberto, *El dilema del Chavismo: una incógnita en el poder*, José Agustín Catalá, Caracas, 1998

Blanco Muñoz, Agustín, *Habla el comandante, testimonios violentos*, UCV, Caracas, 1998

Boustany, Nora, 'Venezuela's Aspiring Innovator', *Washington Post*, Friday 24 September 1999

Bravo, Douglas, y Argelia Melet, *La otra crisis, otra história, otro camino*, Oríjinal Editores, Caracas, 1991

Briceño Porras, Guillermo, *El extraordinário Simón Rodríguez*, Caracas, 1991

Brito Figueroa, Federíco, *Tiempo de Ezequiel Zamora*, José Agustín Catalá, Caracas, 1995

Britto García, Luís, *El poder sin la máscara: de la concertación populista a la explosión social*, 2da edicion, Alfadil Ediciones, Caracas, 1989

Buxton, Julia and Nicola Phillips, *Case Studies in Latin American Political Economy*, Manchester University Press, 1999

Castañeda, Jorge, *Utopia Unarmed: the Latin American Left after the Cold War*, Random House, New York, 1994

Castro, Orlando, *Orlando Castro*, Editora Anexo, Caracas, 1998

Coppedge, Michael, *Strong Parties and Lame Ducks: presidential partyarchy and factionalism in Venezuela*, Stanford University Press, 1994

Coroníl, Fernando, *The Magical State: nature, money and modernity in Venezuela*, University of Chicago Press, 1997

Dieterich, Heinz, *Hugo Chávez: con Bolívar y el Pueblo, nace un nuevo proyecto latinoamericano*, Editorial 21, Buenos Aires, 1999

Ewell, Judith, *Venezuela: a century of change*, Hurst and Co, London, 1984

Garrido, Alberto, *Guerrilla y conspiración militar en Venezuela*, José Agustín Catalá, Caracas, 1999

Giordani, Jorge A, *La propuesta del MAS*, UCV, Caracas, 1992

Gott, Richard, *Guerrilla Movements in Latin America*, Thomas Nelson, London, 1971

Grüber Odreman, Hernán, *Antecedentes históricos de la insurrección militar del 27-N-1992*, Caracas, 1993

Henry, James, *Banqueros y lavadolares: el papel de la banca internacional en la deuda del Tercer Mundo, la fuga de capitales, la corrupción y el antidesarrollo*, Tercer Mundo Editores, Bogota, 1996

Iglesias, María Cristina, *Salto al futuro: conversaciones con Pablo Medina (y otros)*, Ediciones Piedra, Papel o Tijera, Caracas, 1998

Kornblith, Míriam, *Venezuela en los 90: las crisis de la democracia*, Ediciones IESA, Caracas, 1998

Krehm, William, *Democracies and Tyrannies of the Caribbean*, Lawrence Hill & Co, Westport, 1984

Ledezma, Eurídice, Crísis política y nacionalismo, en Venezuela, Mexico, y Peru: un estudio comparado, unpublished thesis, Universidad Complutense de Madrid, 1998

López Maya, Margarita (ed.), *Lucha popular, democracia, neoliberalismo: protesta popular en America Latina en los años de ajuste*, Editorial Nueva Sociedad, Caracas, 1999

López Maya, Margarita, 'El Ascenso en Venezuela de la Causa R,' *Revista Venezolano de Economia y Ciencias Sociales*, UCV, Caracas, 2–3, 1995

McCoy, J. (ed.), *Venezuelan Democracy under Pressure*, North–South Centre, New Brunswick, 1995

Martínez Galindo, Román, *Ezequiel Zamora y la batalla de Santa Inés (prologo Hugo Chávez)*, Vadell Hermanos, Caracas, 1992

Medina, Pablo, *Rebeliones*, Caracas, 1999

Moleiro, Moisés, *El poder y el sueño*, Editorial Planeta Venezolano, Caracas, 1998

Müller Rojas, Alberto, *Relaciones peligrosas: militares, política y estado*, Fondo Editorial Tropykos, Caracas, 1992

Naím, Moisés, *Paper Tigers and Minotaurs: the politics of Venezuela's economic reforms*, Carnegie Endowment, Washington, 1993

Olavarría, Jorge, *El efecto Venezuela*, 3ra edicion, Editorial Panapo, Caracas, 1996

Olavarría, Jorge, *Historia viva: articulos publicados en El Nacional, marzo 1998–marzo 1999*, Caracas, 1999

Peña, Alfredo, *Conversaciones con José Vicente Rangel*, Editorial Ateneo de Caracas, Caracas, 1978

Ramírez Rojas, Kléber, *Historia documental del 4 de febrero*, UCV, Caracas, 1998

Rodríguez, Simón, *Sociedades Americanas*, Biblioteca Ayacucho, Caracas, 1990

Rodríguez-Valdés, Angel, *Los rostros del golpe*, Alfadil Ediciones, Caracas, 1992

Romero, Celino, 'Pacific Revolution', *The World Today* (London), vol. 25, no. 10, October 1999

Santodomingo, Roger, *La conspiración 98: un pacto secreto para llevar a Hugo Chávez al poder*, Alfadil Ediciones, Caracas, 1999

Stepan, Alfred, *The State and Society: Peru in comparative perspective*, Princeton University Press, 1978

Tarre Briceño, Gustavo, *El espejo roto: 4F 1992*, Editorial Panapo, Caracas, 1994

Vivas, Leonardo, *Chávez: la última revolución del siglo*, Editorial Planeta Venezolano, Caracas, 1999

Williamson, John (ed.), *The Political Economy of Reform*, Institute for International Economics, Washington, 1994

Zago, Angela, *La rebelión de los Angeles*, Fuentes Editores, Caracas, 1992

Zapata, Juan Carlos, *Los ricos bobos*, Alfadil Ediciones, Caracas, 1995

INDEX